Europe on the Brink, 1914

REACTING CONSORTIUM PRESS

This book is a "reacting" game. Reacting games
are interactive role-playing games in which students
are responsible for their own learning. Reacting games
are currently used at more than 400 colleges
and universities in the United States and abroad.
Reacting Consortium Press is a publishing program
of the Reacting Consortium, the association of schools
that use reacting games. Barnard College is the host
institution for the Reacting Consortium and Reacting
Consortium Press. For more information visit
http://reactingconsortiumpress.org.

Europe on the Brink, 1914

THE JULY CRISIS

JOHN E. MOSER

Set in Utopia and The Sans

by Westchester Publishing Services

ISBN 978-1-4696-5986-2 (pbk.: alk. paper)

ISBN 978-1-4696-5987-9 (ebook)

Cover illustration: Satirical map of World War I entitled "The Insane Asylum (Old Song, New Tune)" by Louis Raemaekers (1869–1956).

Distributed by the

University of North Carolina Press

116 South Boundary Street

Chapel Hill, NC 27514-3808

www.uncpress.org

Contents

4. ROLES AND FACTIONS / 33

5. CORE TEXTS / 36

Europe on the Brink, 1914

1

Introduction

In *Europe on the Brink, 1914*, students portray political and military leaders of the European powers and must decide how they (and their governments) will respond to the assassination of Archduke Franz Ferdinand, the heir to the throne of Austria-Hungary. In that capacity they will decide within their factions whether the crisis can be settled peacefully; if not, whether to enter the war or remain on the sidelines; and whether, how, and against whom to mobilize their armed forces. If war breaks out, the decisions made by the participants will have a direct effect on the course of the war in its initial months.

Players' decisions will be influenced by a number of important texts related to international relations, including works by Emer de Vattel, Richard Cobden, Heinrich von Treitschke, Giuseppe Mazzini, Nikolai Danilevskii, Norman Angell, and Friedrich von Bernhardi. Excerpts from all of these are included in this gamebook.

The main intellectual clash in the game is between "balance of power" and nationalism. The former had been championed by European states-men since the eighteenth century and was re-garded as the best means for maintaining a stable international system that protected the sovereign rights of each state. The latter emerged in the late eighteenth century and gained strength through the nineteenth. Nationalists regarded ethnicity as the most important source of group identification for individuals and claimed that each sovereign "nation" deserved a government of its own choosing. While early nationalists such as Giuseppe Mazzini remained focused on national unification, later ones such as Nikolai Danilevskii and Fried-rich von Bernhardi embraced a far more expansive vision of national interest, one that justified aggressive wars aimed at asserting the greatness and power of the nation-state. For these later nationalists, concepts such as the balance of power or international law were nothing more than tools used by weaker states to hold back the strong.

PROLOGUE

Sunday, June 28, 1914
The Orient Express

As you deposit your luggage in your sleeping compartment, you feel the jolt as the train begins its departure from Paris's *Gare de l'Est*. The train is crowded with people returning from weekend holidays, so you make your way to the saloon car for a drink, hoping to pick up some of the latest gossip.

You were in Paris as a correspondent for the Hearst newspapers, covering what everyone was calling *l'Affaire Caillaux*—the "crime of the century." In March, Henriette Caillaux, Parisian socialite and wife of Finance Minister Joseph Caillaux, visited the office of Gaston Calmette, editor of the venerable newspaper *Le Figaro*.

Calmette, a critic of J. Caillaux, had obtained some of the finance minister's political correspondence and embarrassed him by publishing it. Henriette feared that Calmette might publish letters of an even more personal nature, showing that she and Joseph had been involved romantically with one another years before their marriage—when in fact they were both married to other people. When she went to see Calmette on March 16, she did so with a concealed .32 Browning automatic pistol on her person. After a brief exchange of words, she drew the weapon and fired six rounds at the editor. Four of them found their mark, killing Calmette. Mme. Caillaux's trial is slated to begin next month; rumor has it that her lawyer will plead her innocence on the grounds that it was a *crime passionnel*. How utterly French.

You had just managed to secure a reasonably cheap apartment in Paris when you got wind of another potentially big story: the archduke Franz Ferdinand, heir to the throne of the Austro-Hungarian Empire, had been shot and killed along with his wife while on an official visit to Sarajevo. *L'Affaire Caillaux* could wait. You bought a ticket to Vienna and set out that same day on the famed Orient Express.

Once inside the saloon car, you order a whiskey neat, and you're lucky enough to find a place to sit. Three gentlemen are seated nearby, engaged in a rather heated conversation in French. Fortunately, you're fluent—fluent enough to pick up on the fact that one of them speaks with an English accent, and another with a German one. The third has a patois that you associate with Alsace, a province that was at one time French but that has been part of Germany since 1871. No wonder they're arguing—nobody hates Germans like Alsatian Frenchmen. The subject of the conversation is the assassination of the archduke. You listen in, hungry for details.

"They say the killer is a Serbian terrorist," says the German—let's call him "Fritz." "It is a well-known fact that the Serbian government has long been driven by hatred of Austria-Hungary. Can there be any doubt that Belgrade is behind this outrage?"

The Frenchman—we'll call him "Pierre"—makes a face. "Such a conclusion is not warranted. A government can't be responsible for every single thing that one of its citizens does."

"Yes," agrees the Englishmen, whom we'll call "Thomas." "I've been to that part of Europe, and I can tell you that nationalism runs deep there. Secret societies abound. And while I won't condone such a savage act as murder, one can't help but feel a bit of sympathy for the Serbs—after all, five million of their countrymen live in Austria-Hungary. Is there any doubt that they'd prefer to live under a Serbian ruler, rather than a German one?"

Fritz snorts. "Serbians are savages. It wasn't that long ago that they killed their own king and queen.

Now they've gone too far, and must be punished. The honor of Austria-Hungary is at stake. But let's not forget Russia's role in all this."

"Russia's role?" Pierre asks, cocking an eyebrow. "Be careful, monsieur, that you do not insult an ally of the French Republic."

"Do not be naïve," the German quips. "The Russians have been stirring up trouble in the Balkans for years. They were behind the formation of the Balkan League back in 1912. They want to cause as much trouble for Austria-Hungary as they can. They look forward to the day when the empire falls apart, so they can set up reliable satellite states among the Slavic populations of Central Europe."

Now Thomas speaks up. "You must be joking. The collapse of Austria-Hungary would bring chaos to that part of Europe, and none of the Great Powers wants to see that. Too many investments are at stake."

"Bah," Pierre chimes in. "Germans are always trying to sow discord between us and our allies. Remember the fuss they made over Morocco in 1905 and 1911? But that didn't work out so well for you, did it? Today England and France are closer than ever."

Thomas looks uncomfortable. "Well, I don't think it's quite correct to say that we are allies. Good friends, perhaps."

"Morocco?" Fritz snaps. "You want to bring up Morocco, where you French and English banded together like thieves to rob Germany of its legitimate interests? This is what you and the Russians have been up to for the last ten years—denying the German people their rightful place in the world—or, as the kaiser put it, our place in the sun."

"Now wait one moment," says Thomas. "While it is true that there is an alliance between France and Russia, there is no such arrangement between those countries and England. We have no more than a series of understandings concerning colonial matters."

"So, then, what would happen if a war were to break out between France and Germany?" Fritz fires back.

"You're asking me to address hypotheticals, of course," replies Thomas. "We would naturally think first and foremost of our national interests, and, as always, those lie in the upholding of the balance of power. We cannot allow Germany to dominate Europe any more than we could allow France to do so under Napoleon."

"Balance of power." Fritz repeats the words scornfully. "That's nothing more than a phrase that you English always trot out to justify your meddling in the affairs of the European continent. If you were really concerned about this 'balance of power,' you wouldn't be flirting with the Russians, who stand poised to overrun Europe and Asia. Have you ever read the work of Nikolai Danilevskii? He laid it all out back in the 1870s. It's called pan-Slavism—all the Slavs of Europe living together in a single gigantic confederation spanning from Central Europe to the Pacific Ocean. The final passing of power from the West to the East. But rather than standing alongside Germany and Austria-Hungary in the defense of Western Civilization, you English and French are helping Russia to tear it down! And for what? To begrudge us a few colonies in Africa?" He turns to Pierre. "To get back Alsace-Lorraine?"

At that Pierre stands up abruptly, obviously struggling to contain his anger. "To you, Alsace-Lorraine may be a trifle. To me, it is not. I was born in Alsace, like our President Poincaré. I was only a boy when German troops marched into our town. It was the only time I recall seeing my father cry. We moved away rather than be ruled over as if we were Africans. Mark my words, monsieur—we French do not want war, but neither shall we shrink from one if you push it upon us. And if you do, Alsace and Lorraine will once again be French!"

He slams down his glass and storms out. Fritz remains behind only a few minutes as he finishes his drink and mutters under his breath. Then he too rises to his feet and walks away without a word.

Thomas notices you staring. "American?" he asks. You haven't said a word, but Europeans somehow always know.

"Yes," you answer. "Do you think there will be a war?"

Thomas waves his hand. "Don't be absurd. A war over the murder of an Austrian nobleman in a city most people in our countries have never heard of? Assassinations are hardly even newsworthy any more. Kaiser Franz Josef's own wife was stabbed to death by an Italian about fifteen years ago. And wasn't your President McKinley killed around the same time?"

You need more convincing. "That was different. They were murdered by anarchists with no ties to foreign governments. And your friends there looked like they were about to start fighting on this train."

"Nationalism and liquor," Thomas responds breezily. "A heady combination. A Frenchman and a German will always find something to squabble over, but wars are a thing of the past. We Europeans have outgrown them."

"How do you figure?"

"There's a book that came out a few years ago by a man named Angell. *The Great Illusion*, it was called. War is a thing of the past, because it's so bloody bad for business. Look at the French and the Germans. Much as they claim to hate one another, the great steel works of the Saar Valley run thanks to French iron ore and German coal. Without both, the mills would cease to function. Meanwhile the Germans drink French wine, while the French drink German beer. A war would prevent the people of Europe from getting what they want. Why do you think we haven't had a war since 1871, or a major European war since the days of Napoleon? Trust me, this will all blow over in a week or so."

"Do you really think so?"

"Absolutely. Besides, there are far more important things going on in the world. The French are preoccupied with this Caillaux trial. There are massive labor struggles taking place in Germany and Russia. And right now, His Majesty's government is trying to keep a civil war from breaking out in Ireland."

"That's comforting, I suppose."

"And if this Serbia thing *does* look like it's getting a bit out of hand, my government will call an international conference, and the professional diplomats will smooth things over. Lord Grey, our foreign secretary, is good at that sort of thing. Now, if you'll excuse me, I have an appointment in Munich tomorrow, and I need to return to my compartment to read over my notes. Good evening."

You return the salutation and watch as he exits the car. You hope the Englishman is right, but even if he's wrong, there is little reason for Americans to be concerned about a war on the other side of the Atlantic. Indeed, it could be very good for your career; folks back home love to read about other people's wars.

You turn to the bartender and motion for another whiskey. It's a long way to Vienna.

HOW TO PLAY THIS GAME

This is a "reacting" game. Reacting games are complex role-playing games, used to teach about moments in history. Students are given elaborate game books, which place them in moments of historical controversy and intellectual ferment. The class becomes a public body of some sort; students, in role, become particular persons from the period, often as members of a faction. Their purpose is to advance a policy agenda and achieve their victory objectives. To do so, they will undertake research and write speeches and position papers, and they will give formal speeches, participate in informal debates and negotiations, and otherwise work to win the game. After a few preparatory lectures, the game begins and the players are in charge; the instructor serves as adviser or "gamemaster." Outcomes sometimes differ from the actual history; a postmortem session at the end of the game sets the record straight.

The following is an outline of what you will encounter in reacting games and what you will be expected to do. While these elements are typical of every reacting game, it is important to remember that every game has its own special quirks.

Game Setup

Your instructor will spend some time before the beginning of the game helping you to understand the historical background. During the setup period, you will read several different kinds of material:

- The game book (from which you are reading now), which includes historical information, rules and elements of the game, and essential documents; and
- Your role, which describes the historical person you will play in the game.

You may also be required to read primary and secondary sources outside the gamebook (perhaps including one or more accompanying books), which provide additional information and arguments for use during the game. Often you will be expected to conduct research to bolster your papers and speeches.

Read all of this contextual material and all of these documents and sources before the game begins. And just as important, go back and reread these materials throughout the game. A second reading while *in role* will deepen your understanding and alter your perspective: ideas take on a different aspect when seen through the eyes of a partisan actor.

Players who have carefully read the materials and who know the rules of the game will invariably do better than those who rely on general impressions and uncertain recollections.

Game Play

Once the game begins, certain players preside over the class sessions. These presiding officers may be elected or appointed. Your instructor then becomes the gamemaster (GM) and takes a seat in the back of the room. While not in control, the GM may do any of the following:

- Pass notes to spur players to action;
- Announce the effects of actions taken inside the game on outside parties (e.g., neighboring

countries) or the effects of outside events on game actions (e.g., a declaration of war); and

- Interrupt and redirect proceedings that have gone off track.

Presiding officers may act in a partisan fashion, speaking in support of particular interests, but they must observe basic standards of fairness. As a failsafe device, most reacting games employ the "Podium Rule," which allows a player who has not been recognized to approach the podium and wait for a chance to speak. Once at the podium, the player has the floor and must be heard.

In order to achieve your objectives, outlined in your role sheet, you must persuade others to support you. You must speak with others, because never will a role contain all that you need to know, and never will one faction have the strength to prevail without allies. Collaboration and coalition-building are at the heart of every game.

Most role descriptions contain secret information which you are expected to guard. Exercise caution when discussing your role with others. You may be a member of a faction, which gives you allies who are generally safe and reliable, but even they may not always be in total agreement with you.

In games where factions are tight-knit groups with fixed objectives, finding a persuadable ally can be difficult. Fortunately, every game includes roles that are undecided (or "indeterminate") about certain issues. Everyone is predisposed on certain issues, but most players can be persuaded to support particular positions. Cultivating these players is in your interest. (By contrast, if you are assigned an "indeterminate" role, you will likely have considerable freedom to choose one or another side in the game; but often, too, indeterminates have special interests of their own.)

Cultivate friends and supporters. Before you speak at the podium, arrange to have at least one supporter second your proposal, come to your defense, or admonish those in the body not paying attention. Feel free to ask the presiding officer to assist you, but appeal to the GM only as a last resort.

Immerse yourself in the game. Regard it as a way to escape imaginatively from your usual "self"—and your customary perspective as a college student in the twenty-first century. At first, this may cause discomfort because you may be advocating ideas that are incompatible with your own beliefs. You may also need to take actions that you would find reprehensible in real life. Remember that a reacting game is only a game and that you and the other players are merely playing roles. When the other players offer criticisms, they are not criticizing you as a person. Similarly, you must never criticize another *person* in the game. But you will likely be obliged to criticize their *persona*. (For example, never say, "Sally's argument is ridiculous." But feel free to say, "Governor Winthrop's argument is ridiculous"—and you would do well to explain exactly why! Always assume, when spoken to by a fellow player—whether in class or out of class—that that person is speaking to you in role.

Help to create this world by avoiding the colloquialisms and familiarities of today's college life. Never should the presiding officer, for example, open a session with the salutation, "Hi guys." Similarly, remember that it is inappropriate to trade on out-of-class relationships when asking for support within the game. ("Hey, you can't vote against me. We're both on the tennis team!")

Reacting games seek to approximate of the complexity of the past. Because some people in history were not who they seemed to be, so, too, some roles in reacting games may include elements of conspiracy or deceit. (For example, Brutus did not announce to the Roman Senate his plans to assassinate Caesar.) If you are assigned such a role, you must make it clear to everyone that you are merely playing a role. If, however, you find yourself in a situation where you find your role and actions to be stressful or uncomfortable, tell the GM.

Game Requirements

Your instructor will explain the specific requirements for your class. In general, a reacting game will require you to perform several distinct but interrelated activities:

- **Reading:** This standard academic work is carried on more purposefully in a reacting course, since what you read is put to immediate use.
- **Research and Writing:** The exact writing requirements depend on your instructor, but in most cases, you will be writing to persuade others. Most of your writing will take the form of policy statements, but you might also write autobiographies, clandestine messages, newspapers, or after-game reflections. In most cases papers are posted on the class website for examination by others. Basic rules: Do not use big fonts or large margins. Do not simply repeat your position as outlined in your role sheets. You must base your arguments on historical facts as well as ideas drawn from assigned texts—and from independent research. (Your instructor will outline the requirements for footnoting and attribution.) Be sure to consider the weaknesses in your argument and address them; if you do not, your opponents will.
- **Public Speaking and Debate:** Most players are expected to deliver at least one formal speech from the podium (the length of the game and the size of the class will affect the number of speeches). Reading papers aloud is seldom effective. Some instructors may insist that students instead speak freely from notes. After a speech, a lively and even raucous debate will likely ensue. Often the debates will culminate in a vote.
- **Strategizing:** Communication among students is a pervasive feature of reacting games. You should find yourself writing emails, texting, and attending meetings on a fairly regular basis. If you do not, you are being outmaneuvered by your opponents.

Skill Development

A recent Associated Press article on education and employment made the following observations:

> The world's top employers are pickier than ever. And they want to see more than high marks and the right degree. They want graduates with so-called soft skills—those who can work well in teams, write and speak with clarity, adapt quickly to changes in technology and business conditions, and interact with colleagues from different countries and cultures. . . . And companies are going to ever-greater lengths to identify the students who have the right mix of skills, by observing them in role-playing exercises to see how they handle pressure and get along with others . . . and [by] organizing contests that reveal how students solve problems and handle deadline pressure.

Reacting games, probably better than most elements of the curriculum, provide the opportunity for developing these "soft skills." This is because you will be practicing persuasive writing, public speaking, critical thinking, problem-solving, and collaboration. You will also need to adapt to changing circumstances and work under pressure.

COUNTERFACTUALS

Limited number of participants: There were many, many more people involved in the decision-making processes of the great powers in 1914 than are represented in the game. To keep the required number of players to a manageable level, the group of people involved has been reduced to a handful of individuals for each country. Not only do they represent the most important figures in European governments; they represent the range of views that would have been found within those governments.

No ambassadors: Historically, ambassadors played a critical role in the negotiations. Rarely did government leaders communicate directly with one another; instead, leaders would convey instructions to their ambassadors abroad, who would engage in discussions with the governments of the states to which they were posted and then report back to their own leadership. In the process communications would often be distorted, sometimes accidentally, sometimes intentionally (usually because ambassadors often developed sympathies for the country to which they were posted). Because this would require many more players—forty if only the five primary powers are used—this element has been eliminated. Players are permitted to send messages directly to other nations' leaders.

Mobilization plans: In many cases, the debates in the game over how best to mobilize each country's armies would have been resolved in the years preceding the July Crisis. They are included in the game to provide a better sense of how these plans influenced the way that the war developed.

Pulitzer Prize: If journalists are used in the game, they will be competing for the 1914 Pulitzer Prize for news reporting. In fact, there was no such thing in 1914, as the Pulitzer Prizes were not awarded until 1917. However, they are included to provide the journalists with a tangible goal.

2

Historical Background

murder of Gaston Calmette by Henriette Caillaux in France.

NARRATIVE

At the time of Archduke Franz Ferdinand's assassination, Europe had not experienced a general war—that is, one that involved all of the great powers—since the final defeat of Napoleon nearly a century before. This is not to say that the period 1815–1914 was entirely peaceful; there were at least a dozen wars fought in Europe (depending on how "war" is defined), and many more waged by individual European powers in Asia, Africa, and elsewhere. However, they all involved fewer than four of the great powers, and tended to be low in intensity and brief in duration. The smallest of these, the Greco-Turkish War of 1897, lasted only thirty days. The largest, the **Crimean War**, was fought between Britain, France, and the Ottoman Empire on one side, and Russia on the other. It lasted two years and four months, but the fighting was almost entirely limited to the Crimean Peninsula, and the vast majority of losses were the result of disease rather than combat.

The nineteenth century was certainly peaceful compared with those that came before and after, but it was not—particularly in its later years—without international animosities. Two very deep antagonisms, in fact, dominated the international politics by 1900. The first was between Germany and France. This was a hatred that went back many years, to a time before there was a Germany, when there was only a highly decentralized Holy Roman Empire of the German Nation that had by turns been aggressor against and victim of encroachment by the French monarchy. It is not surprising, then, that Prussian chancellor Otto von Bismarck saw a war with France as the best means of completing the unification of Germany. In 1870 he got his wish, cleverly goading Paris into declaring war. After defeating the French armies on the battlefield, the German-speaking states of central Europe joined together to form the new German Empire—proclaimed, significantly, at Versailles,

the magnificent palace of the French Sun King, Louis XIV.

But what gave the Franco-German animosity special urgency was that in the treaty that ended the Franco-Prussian War, the provinces of Alsace and Lorraine passed from France to the new Germany. France's historic claims to these territories were not particularly strong; the armies of Louis XIV had taken Alsace from the Holy Roman Empire in the late seventeenth century, and his grandson Louis XV seized Lorraine in the mid-eighteenth. However, the French-speaking population of the two provinces grew rapidly in the subsequent years, so that by 1871 they were, at least linguistically, solidly French.

This was a matter of particular importance, since the nineteenth century was the great age of European **nationalism**. Intellectual, cultural, and political figures across the continent believed that language and ethnicity provided individuals with their strongest ties to one another. By the same token, linguistic and cultural differences—believed to be rooted in blood rather than custom—were regarded as creating natural boundaries between peoples. The nation, then, was thought to be a natural entity that was logically prior to, and hence more important than, superficial political entities. In the eyes of nationalists, Europe's political boundaries should correspond with national ones. Nothing, they believed, was more unnatural than for people of the same ethnicity to live in separate states, or for the people of one nation to be ruled by those of another. Support for nationalism among Europe's educated middle classes was critical to the unification of Italy in 1859–60, and Germany in 1870–71. By the same token, French nationalists would never reconcile themselves to German rule over Alsace-Lorraine.

In the short term, however, there was nothing that Paris could do to alter this situation, as skillful diplomacy by Bismarck (now chancellor not just of Prussia, but all of Germany) succeeded in keeping France isolated. The new German Empire joined with Russia and Austria-Hungary to form the Three Emperors' Alliance (Dreikaiserbund) in 1873, and concluded the **Triple Alliance** with Austria-Hungary and Italy in 1882. With Great Britain enjoying "splendid isolation" from European affairs—and, in fact, repeatedly coming into conflict with France as the two powers sought to colonize Africa—there was not a single major power in Europe willing to align itself with Paris for nearly two decades.

The fact that this state of affairs did not last stems almost entirely from Europe's other great animosity, between Russia and Austria-Hungary. Russia had long regarded itself as the protector of the Eastern Orthodox peoples (often, but not always, of Slavic descent) of the Balkan peninsula, who had for centuries lived under Islamic rule in the form of the Ottoman Empire (based on modern-day Turkey). This had led to a series of Russo-Turkish wars in the seventeenth, eighteenth, and nineteenth centuries. Early on, these had not generated much tension with Austria; indeed, the two countries on several occasions fought as allies against the Ottoman Turks. But by the early nineteenth century, the Ottoman Empire was in obvious decline, opening up the possibility of significant Russian gains in the region.

From the perspective of Austria (Austria-Hungary from 1867) and its Habsburg emperors, Russian expansion in southeastern Europe was threatening for two reasons. First, they believed that it jeopardized one of the most important principles of international relations during this period, the **balance of power**. It was an idea that was first articulated in the early eighteenth century, but its theorists claimed to see it in play even in the days of Ancient Greece. According to balance-of-power thinking, peace was best preserved when no state became so powerful that it could menace the independence of the others; any monarch who tried to do so had to be resisted by a coalition of enemies dedicated to restoring the equilibrium. This, they argued, was precisely what happened when Louis XVI and Napoleon tried to

achieve dominance over Europe. Belief in a balance of power naturally led governments to eye their neighbors warily, looking for any sign that they might be growing too powerful. It encouraged the formation of alliances, in which countries sought to counterbalance their rivals. In addition, whenever one state defeated another in a war, it became common for third powers to intervene in an effort to limit the victor's territorial gains, or to seek compensation elsewhere. As Ottoman control over the Balkans receded, then, the Habsburgs worried that Russia would become the dominant force in the region.

Austria was also concerned about Russian policy in southeastern Europe because St. Petersburg was actively encouraging nationalism in that region. As Ottoman power retreated, independent Greek, Serbian, Romanian, and Bulgarian states emerged over the course of the century. Some of these states came to view Russia as their natural protector, as many Russian nationalists embraced the idea of **pan-Slavism**: that is, the belief that all the Slavic peoples of eastern Europe should be united in a single confederation.

Russian support for pan-Slavism was deeply worrying to the Habsburgs because of all the great powers, the Habsburg Empire was the only one not built on the national principle. To be sure, Germany had significant Polish, Danish, and (thanks to its control of Alsace-Lorraine) French minorities, and a great many non-Russians lived within the borders of the Russian Empire. The Habsburg Monarchy, however, had formed over centuries as diverse territories gradually came under the control of Vienna. The empire's ruling family may have been German, but its population consisted of a bewildering array of peoples—Germans, Hungarians, Poles, Ukrainians, Czechs, Slovaks, Serbs, Croatians, Romanians, Slovenians, and Italians, just to name the largest. No single ethnic group possessed anything close to a majority. Therefore, unlike in places such as France or Germany, where the national principle served as a source of unity and strength, nationalism in Austria could only promote fragmentation. Indeed, the Habsburgs had managed to keep the Hungarians from leaving the empire altogether only by forging a compromise (*Ausgleich*) in 1867, in which the Austrian Empire became the Austro-Hungarian Empire—two separate "nations," each with its own parliament, united only in the person of the emperor. If other ethnic groups were to assert themselves in the same way, the empire might dissolve entirely.

Habsburg worries over Russian power and Balkan nationalism manifested themselves as early as the middle of the century. During the Crimean War, the Austrian emperor, the young **Franz Josef I**, earned Russian enmity by threatening to intervene on the side of the French and British if Russian troops were not withdrawn from the Black Sea provinces of Moldavia and Wallachia (modern-day Romania). Nearly fifty years later, when Tsar Alexander II sought to create a huge (pro-Russian) Kingdom of Bulgaria in the Balkans after the Russo-Turkish War of 1877–78, Austria-Hungary joined with Britain and France to demand that the tsar moderate his gains. Bismarck, declaring Germany to be nothing more than an "honest broker," hosted an international congress in Berlin in which Russia was obliged to accept a smaller Bulgaria, and Austria-Hungary, as compensation for Russian gains, was granted the right to occupy and administer the Ottoman provinces of Bosnia and Herzegovina.

The tensions between Austria-Hungary and Russia ultimately doomed Bismarck's Dreikaiserbund, which was finally allowed to lapse in 1887. Germany remained allied to Austria-Hungary via the Triple Alliance, but Bismarck still attempted to maintain the relationship with Russia through a three-year Reinsurance Treaty, in which each power promised to remain neutral if the other became involved in a war with a third party. However, the chancellor resigned in 1890, and when Russia soon afterward sought to renew the treaty, the young German emperor (kaiser), **Wilhelm II**, said no. The immediate beneficiary of this decision was France, which was finally able to end its diplomatic isolation by concluding an alliance with Russia in August 1892. This alignment seemed unlikely, inasmuch as it bound together Europe's largest republic with its most autocratic monarchy. It certainly came as a shock to Wilhelm II, a believer in absolute monarchy who never imagined that the archconservative Alexander III of Russia would ever make common cause with the French Republic. Nevertheless, from the standpoint of the balance of power, it made perfect sense, as it provided an effective counterweight to the Triple Alliance.

The conclusion of the Franco-Russian military convention left Great Britain as the only major power that did not belong to an alliance. For most of the century, this had not struck the successive governments in power as a problem; indeed, the country's "splendid isolation" from European entanglements was a point of national pride. London had tended to focus instead on its massive global empire. However, it became increasingly difficult to divorce European from colonial affairs in the period after 1880, when the European powers began to help themselves to great chunks of Africa. The so-called "scramble" for Africa placed Britain on a collision course with France, which had long possessed colonial interests in Africa, as well as with Germany, which was just getting into the game. At the same time, the British regarded Russian expansion in Central Asia—deemed all the more important in St. Petersburg after the tsar's Balkan ambitions had been checked at the Congress of Berlin—as a serious threat to their empire in India. When in 1899–1902 the Crown fought a bloody war against the Boers (the descendants of Dutch settlers in South Africa), it briefly appeared as though the French, Germans, and Russians might forget their differences and form a common front against Britain. The Foreign Office concluded that "splendid isolation" was now a liability; the Empire had to find friends on the Continent, and fast.

But to which side should the British turn? Originally there seemed to be a strong argument for aligning with Germany. Historically England had a tradition of siding with the German states against France, which had been a frequent enemy since the Middle Ages; indeed, in the days of Napoleon, the United Kingdom was continuously at war with France for twelve years. Relations with Russia were at least as bad; as mentioned earlier, St. Petersburg's efforts to expand in Central Asia were regarded as dangerous to India, the "jewel in the crown" of the British Empire. There were also cultural ties between the two countries: the current and previous dynasties of the monarchy (the House of Hanover and the House of Saxe-Coburg-Gotha) both came from the German states. For this reason, the two powers engaged in negotiations between 1898 and 1901 for an alliance.

However, such a relationship was not to be. Much of the reason for this was that the dramatic, mercurial Wilhelm II sought to make Germany, already the most powerful country on the European continent, into a world power. Bursting onto the global scene at a time when much of the underdeveloped world had already been colonized, German politicians, diplomats, business leaders, and journalists loudly demanded a "place in the sun." With a large and growing industrial economy, German manufactured goods competed effectively with British products on world markets. The hallmark of a truly great nation, Germans argued, was the possession of colonies, so Germany must receive its share. Even more threatening from the British perspective was Berlin's decision in 1898 to start building a world-class battle fleet. For the British, who were accustomed to having the Royal Navy rule the waves, this seemed like a direct challenge. Soon Germany and Britain were locked in a naval race, and officials in the British Foreign Office were arguing that Germany was a threat to the hallowed balance of power. The logical move, they argued, was to put aside ancient animosities and throw Britain's weight on the side of Russia and France.

In April 1904 Britain and France concluded the Entente Cordiale. It was not an alliance, for it committed neither side to come to the other's aid in time of war. However, it did clear up a number of long-standing colonial disputes between the two powers, most notably in Egypt (where France agreed to recognize British domination) and Morocco (where Britain acknowledged French preponderance). Soon the agreement produced an international crisis, when France attempted to establish a protectorate[1] over Morocco. German firms had significant commercial interests in that country, Wilhelm II personally came to Tangiers to offer his support to the sultan, and for a few days Germany and France seemed poised on the brink of war. The **First Moroccan Crisis** (as we will see, a second followed in 1911) was settled through an international conference, held at Algeciras, Spain, in early 1906. The assembled great powers (including the United States) voted in France's favor, with only Austria-Hungary siding with Germany. French administrators and financiers would be permitted to exercise practical control over the country, although the Moroccan police—and not French troops—would have responsibility for maintaining law and order in the country.

The Entente Cordiale cleared the way for improved relations with Russia as well. In 1907 the two countries signed the **Anglo-Russian Convention**, in which they settled their differences over Persia (which was divided into British and Russian spheres of influence) and Afghanistan. Again, there was no official alliance, but increasingly politicians and journalists began referring to the **Triple Entente**. Wilhelm II and German nationalists were both horrified and outraged, claiming that the three powers were seeking the encirclement (*Einkreisung*) of Germany.

Mere months after the conclusion of the Anglo-Russian Convention, a revolution took place in the

1. A "protectorate" exists when a country keeps—at least in name—its own government, but under the "protection" of another nation. The "protector" normally stations troops in that country, and for all practical purposes controls it.

Ottoman Empire. A group of Turkish nationalists, organized into a party called the Committee of Union and Progress (often referred to as the **"Young Turks"**), forced the sultan, Abdul Hamid II, to accept a constitution that significantly limited his powers. (The sultan was kept under house arrest until the following year, when he was deposed in favor of his younger brother, Mehmed V, who reigned as a figurehead.) The ensuing chaos tempted a whole range of countries to lay claims to parts of the crumbling empire, while others (in true balance-of-power fashion) sought to limit the gains of their rivals or to seek compensation elsewhere.

The first of these emerged that very summer, from a deal concluded between Russia and Austria-Hungary. At a secret meeting at Buchlau Castle (in the modern-day Czech Republic), the Russian foreign minister, Alexander Izvolsky, agreed to support a move by Austria-Hungary formally to annex the provinces of Bosnia and Herzegovina. In return, the Austro-Hungarian foreign minister, Alois Lexa von Aehrenthal, promised to support the right of Russia to move warships through the strategically vital Turkish straits, which linked the Black Sea to the Mediterranean. However, the precise terms remain unclear. Izvolsky would later claim that he had only intended for these issues to be brought before an international congress. He expressed profound shock when, in early October 1908, Kaiser Franz Josef I officially proclaimed Bosnia-Herzegovina to be a province of the Austro-Hungarian Empire. He was also profoundly embarrassed when Aehrenthal announced that the Russian foreign minister had known about it all along.

If the annexation of Bosnia-Herzegovina embarrassed Izvolsky, it outraged Austria-Hungary's neighbor to the south, Serbia. The Principality of Serbia (it became a kingdom in 1882) gained formal independence from the Ottoman Empire in 1878, but for the first twenty-five years of its existence, it had managed to remain on friendly terms with the Habsburg Monarchy. Bulgaria,

which won its independence at the same time, was far more closely aligned with Russia. However, this changed with the brutal assassination of the Serbian king, Alexander I, in 1903. The new monarch, Peter I, came from a rival family and enjoyed the support of nationalists who believed that it was Serbia's historical destiny to unite the so-called South Slavs—the Serbs, Croats, and Slovenes—into a single state. Since most of the South Slavs lived within the borders of Austria-Hungary, this necessarily meant a reversal of Serbia's traditional pro-Habsburg policy. King Peter quickly sought to align his country with Russia, where the growing pan-Slavist movement openly called for the dissolution of the Habsburg Monarchy and the creation of a Slavic Federation in southeastern Europe. When Belgrade began to seek investment from France, Vienna retaliated by closing its borders to Serbian pork, the first shot in a trade war that would last for three years.

Because most of the people who lived in Bosnia-Herzegovina were Serbs and Croats, Serbian nationalists had expected that eventually the territories would come under Belgrade's control. When Franz Josef announced that they would henceforth be Habsburg lands, therefore, Serbia erupted in outrage. Just two days after the announcement, Serbian nationalists formed an organization called **Narodna Odbrana** (Defense of the people), dedicated to the eventual liberation of South Slavs from Austro-Hungarian rule. Over the next six years, the group would wage an incessant propaganda campaign against Vienna, "our first and greatest enemy."

The **Bosnian Crisis** of 1908–9 was the first of a series of incidents in the Balkans that might have resulted in a European war. Serbia mobilized its army, demanding either Bosnia-Herzegovina or compensation elsewhere, and Austria-Hungary followed suit. Belgrade appealed to Russia for support, and Izvolsky was inclined to grant it. However, Germany stood firmly behind its Habsburg allies, while France and Britain were understandably reluctant to back up the Russians over what seemed to them to be a relatively minor matter. Russia was in no position to fight—certainly not without allies—given that only three years earlier it had suffered a humiliating defeat in a war against Japan. Izvolski in late March 1909 reluctantly called on the Serbs to stand down.

Just over two years later a new crisis erupted over Morocco. A rebellion broke out in the country, and insurgents quickly occupied most of the capital, Fez, and surrounded the sultan in his palace. In April 1911 France dispatched troops to Fez to protect the sultan (as well as French investments), leading to immediate protests from Berlin, which claimed that this was a violation of the agreement reached at Algeciras five years earlier. In an effort to assert German interests in the region, Wilhelm II dispatched a warship, which arrived at the Moroccan port of Agadir on July 1. German nationalists responded by calling for war, but it soon became clear that Britain would stand by France in any resulting conflict. Even Chancellor of the Exchequer David Lloyd George, who had a reputation for being pro-German, warned that "if Britain is treated badly where her interests are vitally affected, as if she is of no account in the cabinet of nations, then I say emphatically that peace at that price would be a humiliation intolerable for a great country like ours to endure."[2] Berlin, therefore, sought a diplomatic solution. In the resulting Treaty of Fez, signed in early November, France was granted a full protectorate over Morocco (including the right to station troops there indefinitely), while Germany was compensated with a small strip of territory in central Africa. All in all, the **Agadir Crisis** (sometimes called the Second Moroccan Crisis) demonstrated the strength of the Entente Cordiale, and was regarded by German nationalists as a humiliating retreat.

2. "Agadir Crisis: Lloyd George's Mansion House Speech, 21 July, 1911," World War I Document Archive, http://wwi.lib.byu.edu/index.php/Agadir_Crisis:_Lloyd_George%27s_Mansion_House_Speech.

While the world's attention was focused on Morocco, Italy took advantage of Ottoman weakness by launching an attack against Turkish territory in North Africa and the Dodecanese Islands. Following traditional balance-of-power logic, Rome was convinced that if Italy were to be regarded as a great power, it would need to make gains comparable to those made recently by France in Morocco and Austria-Hungary in Bosnia-Herzegovina. In many ways the **Italo-Turkish War of 1911–12** was a foreshadowing of the kind of fighting that would be seen in World War I. Both sides resorted to trench warfare, and the conflict saw the first use in combat of armored cars and aircraft. By December the fighting had resulted in stalemate, but the Ottoman Empire was in no condition to wage a long war. In October 1912 the two sides concluded the Treaty of Lausanne, under which Libya became part of the Italian Empire. The Dodecanese Islands were to be returned to Turkish control, but three years later they were still occupied by Italian troops.

Perhaps the main reason why the Turks were willing to come to terms with Italians was the fact that they now had to deal with an attack from another direction. For years the Russian minister to Belgrade, Nicolas Hartwig, had been pushing for an alliance among the Balkan states. Hartwig, an ardent pan-Slavist, had taken up his post in the wake of the Bosnian Crisis, and he saw such an arrangement as a way to promote Russian interests in the region while undermining those of Austria-Hungary. His efforts bore fruit in March 1912, when Serbia and Bulgaria concluded an alliance, and in the next few months Montenegro and Greece joined as well. However, instead of targeting the Habsburgs, the new Balkan League cast its eyes on the Ottoman Empire's remaining territory in Europe. With the government in Constantinople still embroiled in war with Italy, the countries of the league saw an opportunity for quick gains.

The **First Balkan War** began in early October 1912, and over the course of a few months the Balkan League succeeded in driving Ottoman forces from the peninsula. The Bulgarian Army defeated the main Turkish army and captured the city of Adrianople (Edirne), while the Serbians marched south into Macedonia, entering Skopje. The Greeks, meanwhile, occupied Salonika and Ioannina. These stunning defeats led to a coup in Constantinople, as a triumvirate of leading members of the Committee of Union and Progress—who would soon come to be known as the **"Three Pashas"**—ousted the reigning ministers and seized power for themselves. But the change of regime made no practical difference on the battlefield, and by early spring the Three Pashas were signaling their desire for peace. In the Treaty of London, signed on May 30, 1913, the Turks formally recognized the loss of all of their European territory, aside from Constantinople itself and a small strip of land to the west of the city. Almost immediately, however, the victorious allies began arguing over the division of the spoils, the Bulgarians arguing that their defeat of the main Ottoman army entitled them to a larger share. In June Serbia and Greece concluded a new alliance, and at the end of that month Bulgarian troops attacked Serbian forces in Macedonia. In this **Second Balkan War** the Bulgarians soon found themselves overmatched, as Romania joined the war on the Greco-Serbian side, and even the Turks took the opportunity to try to win back some of what they had lost by attacking Bulgaria from the east. In early August the belligerents came to terms, with Bulgaria forced to give up much of what it had claimed, and Greece and Serbia dividing Macedonia between themselves. Romania also gained some territory at Bulgaria's expense, while the Ottoman Empire regained Adrianople.

Vienna observed the events of the Balkan Wars with dismay. The willingness of the Balkan states to join together (if only temporarily) was upsetting enough; the fact that Serbia, mortal enemy of the Habsburgs, roughly doubled in size as a result of its conquests was even more troubling. During the peace negotiations in London, Austria-Hungary insisted on the creation of a new state of Albania,

mainly so that Serbia would be denied some of its military gains (and access to the Adriatic Sea). Enraged, Belgrade for a time refused to withdraw its forces from the region and found a sympathetic ear among pan-Slavs at the court of Tsar **Nicholas II** in St. Petersburg. Austria-Hungary mobilized its army, and Germany promised full support for Vienna. For a moment Europe stood on the brink of war; however, Russia was still recovering from its defeat by Japan in 1905–6, and neither Britain nor France had any desire to be drawn into the affair. Serbia, on orders from St. Petersburg, stood down a second time.

A few months later, still another crisis flared up in the East, this time occasioned by the announcement by the Ottoman government of the Three Pashas in early November that a retired German general, Otto Liman von Sanders, was to assume command of the Turkish First Army, charged with protecting Constantinople. While it was not unusual for foreign officers to serve as advisers to the Turks (indeed, a British admiral was at that time serving in that capacity in the Ottoman Navy), for such a person to be placed in actual charge of military forces was unprecedented. Russia immediately cried foul, with Foreign Minister Sergei Sazonov warning that this would be regarded in St. Petersburg as an "openly hostile act." Since so much of Russian trade moved through the Black Sea Straits, Constantinople was not merely a matter of Turkish concern; indeed, during the Italo-Turkish War the Ottomans had closed the straits to all foreign traffic, dealing a serious blow to the Russian economy. The **Liman von Sanders Affair** might have led to war between Germany and Russia had a face-saving solution not been found—the general, instead of being given command of the First Army Corps, was appointed inspector-general of the Turkish Army in January 1914.

At the same time when the Liman von Sanders Affair complicated Germany's relations with Russia, a domestic political crisis increased tensions with France. In the small French-speaking town of Zabern (today Saverne) in Alsace-Lorraine (which, it will be recalled, was annexed by Germany after the Franco-Prussian War), there was open hostility between the local populace and the German garrison. In late October a Prussian officer advised his men, "If you are attacked, use your weapon, and if you stab a *Wackes* in the process, then you'll get ten marks from me," and his words were promptly leaked to the local newspapers. The officer's suggestion that violence be employed against the townsfolk was bad enough; that he used the ethnic slur *Wackes* (which roughly translates as "square head") made it even worse, and from all over Alsace-Lorraine there came demands for disciplinary action. The **Zabern Affair** brought to the surface the deep-seated hostility between French and German nationalists, but it had a domestic component as well. Even the Reichstag (the German legislature) called for the officer to be punished, but the German Army's refusal to comply suggested to the world that the armed forces were not subject to civilian authority. *Every country had*

Despite this series of events, in spring 1914 *their problem* virtually no one believed in the likelihood of a general European war. Part of this lack of concern stemmed from the fact that foreign affairs rarely managed to capture the attention of either elites or the public the way that domestic matters did. Nearly all of the major powers in 1914 were in the midst of political crises that dominated the newspaper headlines. In Germany the Social Democratic Party, which openly embraced Marxism, had emerged in the 1912 Reichstag elections as the largest political party in the country. Some on the right responded by calling for a "national dictatorship" involving the imposition of martial law, bans on left-wing political organizations and newspapers, a closing of the Reichstag, and a purge of Jews from education, the civil service, and the army. By early 1914 the kaiser's own son, Crown Prince Wilhelm, had emerged as the informal leader of these reactionary forces.[3]

Russia, meanwhile, was the scene of intense labor struggles in 1914, as workers and peasants alike expressed their dissatisfaction with their living and working conditions. The growing industrial sector was paralyzed by a series of strikes—roughly one million factory laborers walked off their jobs at some point during the first half of the year. In the countryside newspapers reported an upsurge in murders, assaults, plundering of crops, and burning of noble-owned manors. In times of crisis Russians were accustomed to looking to their tsar, who ruled as virtually an absolute monarch in an age in which the balance of political power in most countries (even Germany) was tipping in favor of elected legislatures. But the current occupant of the throne, Nicholas II, was widely believed to have come under the influence of a half-mad monk, a self-proclaimed "holy man" named Rasputin. "If I am not there to protect you," the monk allegedly warned the terrified Tsarina, "you will lose your crown and your son within six months."[4]

France was a deeply divided nation in 1914, and there were widespread concerns that the country was in decline. Its population had only grown from 37 million to 39 million since the Franco-Prussian War (by contrast, German's population has surged from 42 million to 62 million), and the German economy had grown nearly twice as much as the French. Most worrying of all, however, was the chronic chaos that afflicted the French government. Disdainful monarchists were quick to point out that no fewer than eleven governments had come and gone since 1909, four in 1913 alone. Political life and society at large were divided between a traditionalist, aristocratic, deeply Catholic Right and a secular, socialist Left, both of which questioned at times whether the republic was worth defending. In the middle stood the bourgeoisie—the state's only truly reliable defenders. These divisions came through in the 1890s and 1900s in the "**Dreyfus Affair**," in which Alfred

3. Jack Beatty, *The Lost History of 1914: Reconsidering the Year the Great War Began* (New York: Walker, 2012), 39.

4. Beatty, *Lost History of 1914*, 72–73.

Dreyfus, an army officer of Jewish descent, was accused and convicted of selling military secrets to the Germans. Liberals rallied to his defense, and a subsequent investigation established Dreyfus's innocence—as well as the fact that anti-Semitic officers of the French Army had falsified evidence in an effort to convict him.

More recently, France's political divisions reemerged in a spectacular "trial of the century"—that of Henriette Caillaux, wife of Joseph Caillaux, one of the most prominent left-wing (and antiwar) politicians in France. She stood accused of murdering Gaston Calmette, the deeply conservative and nationalistic editor of *Le Figaro*, one of the country's biggest newspapers, in March 1914. Upon hearing of her arrest, Joseph resigned from his post as finance minister. By June all of France was buzzing about the upcoming trial. If Henriette were found guilty, her husband's political career would be finished, but if she were exonerated, he would no doubt return to politics, where he would be a serious thorn in the side of **Raymond Poincaré**, the republic's deeply conservative president.

There were signs of industrial discontent in Austria-Hungary as well, but the most pressing problems facing the Habsburg Monarchy in 1914 were those of ethnicity, not class. The multinational nature of the empire frequently paralyzed the legislature, and fistfights on the floor of the Reichsrat (Austria's parliament) were far from uncommon. But the legislature had little real power. Nearly all the authority lay with the emperor and his ministers, and here it was the relationship between the Austrian and Hungarian halves of the monarchy that was most important. Under the *Ausgleich* (compromise) of 1867 the two sides operated very much like two separate governments, united only in the person of the monarch, Franz Josef. Every ten years the terms of the compromise had to be renewed, and each time the Magyars (the formal name for the ethnic group of Hungarians) threatened to dissolve the union if their demands were not met—and invariably those demands involved (1) limiting the Magyars' contributions to the monarchy's most important common institution, the armed forces, and (2) the Magyars' ability to rule over the millions of non-Hungarians who lived within their borders. The Romanians of Transylvania were a particular target for Magyar suppression, so that just as the South Slavs of Bosnia looked toward Serbia for their salvation, the Romanians increasingly sought relief from the independent Romania that lay just beyond Hungary's eastern border.[5]

It was likely the English who were paying the least attention to matters on the continent of Europe; their minds were instead riveted on Ireland. For much of the late nineteenth century the Liberal Party had been pressing for "**home rule**" for Ireland—that is, self-government within the United Kingdom of Britain and Ireland. In March 1914, thanks to the efforts of Prime Minister **Herbert Asquith**, the goal seemed to be in reach, with Conservatives in the minority in Parliament and King George V expressing his full support. The stumbling block was the status of Ulster, Ireland's six northernmost counties. While the rest of the country was overwhelmingly Catholic, and supportive of home rule, the counties of Ulster had narrow Protestant majorities, and bitterly resisted the thought of being part of an autonomous Catholic Ireland. A paramilitary organization calling itself the Ulster Volunteer Force (UVF) threatened violence if Parliament passed the bill, and British army and navy officers stationed there calmly informed their superiors in London that they had no intention of doing anything to stop it. Catholics responded by forming their own para-

---

5. Many observers believed that the current arrangement of Austria-Hungary was untenable. Some suggested as an alternative a federal union, in which each nationality of the monarchy would possess some level of autonomy in a "United States of Greater Austria." The most determined enemies of such a scheme were the Magyars. Its staunchest advocate was the heir to the Habsburg throne—Archduke Franz Ferdinand.

military units, and by spring 1914 Ireland seemed on the brink of civil war.

But if most Europeans were more interested in domestic matters, neither did the relative few who dutifully followed foreign affairs expect a general war; it had, after all, been nearly a century since the last one. Of course, it was only to be expected that international crises would flare up now and again. But each time, whether the object was Morocco, Bosnia-Herzegovina, Libya, Macedonia, Albania, Constantinople, or little Zabern, the diplomats succeeded time and again in defusing the situation. There was no reason to think that they would not be capable of doing the same in the future. Moreover, there were reasons for optimism about the health of the international system. In particular, Anglo-German relations, soured by the naval race and trade rivalry between the two countries, seemed to be on the mend in the past few years. While the naval race had not exactly ended, German battleship production had been pushed aside in favor of other priorities. Moreover, the two countries cooperated on the question of an independent Albania and the construction of a German railroad connecting Berlin and Baghdad.

There was also a growing peace movement during the late nineteenth and early twentieth centuries, as religious sects, women's groups, and labor organizations opposed to war emerged in each of the great powers. Such organizations frequently corresponded across national lines, holding international congresses in which they pledged to work toward peaceful coexistence. Several left-wing parties, such as France's Socialist Party and the German Social Democratic Party, pledged to resist any effort by their countries' governments to wage war. And before his death in 1896 the Swedish industrialist and armaments manufacturer Alfred Nobel willed a portion of his vast inheritance to go toward an annual prize for the person who had "done the most or the best work for fraternity between nations, for the abolition or reduction of standing armies and for the

holding and promotion of peace congresses." The first **Nobel Peace Prize** was awarded in 1901.

Indeed, some Europeans had begun to believe that major wars had become a thing of the past. In 1909 Norman Angell wrote a small book titled *The Great Illusion*, in which he argued that the industrial economies of the great powers had become so interdependent that any such war would be futile. Because, for example, the German steel industry needed French iron ore, while the French steel industry required German coal, the disruption caused by a war between the two would bring only ruin to both sides. While it is important to note that he never claimed that war had become impossible, he certainly seemed to suggest that no far-seeing statesman would ever choose to start one.

It should be noted that not everyone saw this as a welcome development. The late nineteenth and early twentieth centuries saw the rise of **militarism**, the belief in not only the importance of a strong army and navy but the notion that the armed forces provided a model that the rest of society should emulate. War, militarists argued, brought out the best in young men; in the ranks, individuals sacrificed their selfish desires for the good of the nation as a whole. Long periods of peace, they claimed, caused men to lose their martial spirit and to care for only their own well-being. This point of view, unsurprisingly, was usually strongest among army and navy officers.

Many educated Europeans during this period also embraced the theory of **social Darwinism**, in which nationalism intersected with a particular interpretation of the ideas of the eminent English naturalist Charles Darwin. According to social Darwinism, differences among ethnic groups corresponded to the variations that emerged among the various species and subspecies of the animal kingdom. Such features made some peoples (or "races") more "fit" than others; social Darwinists, in fact, believed in a strict hierarchy of races, inevitably placing their own nationalities among those at the top. Like militarism, social

Darwinism explicitly sanctioned warfare. Since all of nature represented a struggle for survival in a world of limited resources, war was, in the words of the German general Friedrich von Bernhardi, "a biological necessity." Without it there was no effective mechanism by which the weak would be killed off, leaving them to reproduce, thus causing the entire human race to degenerate.

Yet no matter how popular such ideologies might have been in the early twentieth century, most people were not clamoring for war in 1914. Nor did they expect it. When they learned at the end of June that the heir to the Austro-Hungarian throne had been killed, most European statesmen did not even cancel their weekend plans. Assassinations of prominent figures were hardly uncommon during this time. In fact, since 1890 assassins had claimed the lives of an empress of Austria-Hungary, two prime ministers of Bulgaria, a governor general and an attorney general of Finland, a president of France, a prime minister and king of Greece, a king of Italy, a grand vizier of the Ottoman Empire, a king and crown prince of Portugal, two interior ministers and a prime minister of Russia, a king and queen of Serbia, two prime ministers of Spain, and a president of the United States. None of those instances produced a war, or even a serious international crisis. Moreover, if the Moroccan Crisis and the Balkan Wars had failed to trigger a European-wide conflict, there seemed little chance of one occurring over Franz Ferdinand.

Still, the great question remained—would governments and diplomats be able to calm the troubled waters of international politics, as they had so many times before? Or would the murder of the Archduke be the spark that would set Europe ablaze?

3
The Game

Each player portrays a leading figure in the government of one of the European powers in July 1914. In most cases each faction will be made up of one chief executive (a monarch, a president, or a prime minister), a foreign minister, and a military commander (a war minister or an army chief of staff). Unlike many other Reacting games, there is no one setting where the action takes place, unless an international conference is called. Most discussion will take place within factions; contacts between factions are understood to represent telegrams, telephone calls, or meetings with ambassadors.

MAJOR ISSUES FOR DEBATE

Who or what was most responsible for the outbreak of war in 1914? Were there certain individuals who bear a greater share of blame? Certain countries? What about ideologies, such as balance of power, nationalism, social Darwinism, or militarism? What about structural factors, such as the alliance system, or capitalism?

Under what circumstances should a country to go to war—to maintain the balance of power, to satisfy nationalist aspirations, to uphold a particular form of government, to assist allies, to protect smaller countries from aggression, or something else?

What is "national interest"? Is it the interests of the government, the people of a country, people of similar ethnic heritage who live beyond the country's borders, or some other group?

Which is the more effective means of securing national interest—the pursuit of careful diplomacy combined with strict adherence to international law, or reliance on armed might and firm alliances?

Should a country always abide by the terms of treaties, even when those terms no longer serve the national interest?

Is it acceptable to silence, or even jail, dissenters in times of grave national crisis?

RULES AND PROCEDURES

Europe on the Brink, 1914 is primarily a game about negotiations, both intranationally and internationally. Most of the action will take place in groups of three players (one or two for smaller powers), representing the primary decision-makers in each country. For example, the German "faction" is made up of Kaiser Wilhelm I, Chancellor Theobald on Bethmann-Hollweg, and Chief of the General Staff Helmuth von Moltke. In most factions, all national decisions must be agreed to unanimously; however, in the case of Russia and Germany Tsar Nicholas II and Kaiser Wilhelm II, respectively, have the power to force a decision if the other members of the faction are divided. At the same time, players may also send messages to their counterparts in other countries, either to negotiate with hostile powers or to coordinate efforts with allies.

The Austro-Hungarian Response to the Assassination

The first decision that must be made in the game is by the Austro-Hungarian faction—Foreign Minister Leopold Berchtold, Army Chief of Staff Franz Conrad von Hötzendorf, and Hungarian prime minister István Tisza. They must agree unanimously on how to respond to the assassination of Archduke Franz Ferdinand. Normally this will take place outside of class, since the game cannot properly begin until this critical decision has been made and announced to the other players.

Mobilization

The first set of decisions that the Austro-Hungarian, Russian, German, and French factions will have to make concerns mobilization of the armed forces: under what circumstances should they be mobilized, against whom, and in what disposition (i.e., what proportion of the armed forces should be assigned to which fronts)? This will be determined during Game Session 1.

The mobilization of a modern army is a vastly complicated process which involves the calling up of reserves, requisitioning enormous quantities of munitions and supplies, arming and equipping of troops, and movement of men from rallying points throughout the country to the border. It can take anywhere from a few days to many weeks, depending on the country's geographic area, the size of its army, and the state of its railroad network.

The question of whether and when to mobilize is a critical one. Because mobilization takes time, it requires statesmen to look into the future and imagine how circumstances are likely to develop in the next days or weeks. Also, while the specific details of mobilization may be kept secret, the fact that a country is mobilizing is public knowledge. Mobilizing too early could alarm other powers and close off possibilities for negotiations; mobilizing too late could put a country into the difficult position of having to defend itself from attack before its forces are fully deployed.

There are four characters specifically tasked with presenting plans for mobilization: the military commanders Joffre (France), von Moltke (Germany), Sukhomlinov (Russia), and Conrad von Hötzendorf (Austria-Hungary). Other members of their factions are then free to comment on the proposal, and the goal will be to end up with a plan that is acceptable to all members. Once approved, the plan is formally submitted to the gamemaster.

The strength of each country's army is represented abstractly through the use of a number called "Firepower." Each country will have a number of Firepower Points (FPs). These represent not only the size but the overall effectiveness of the military. Thus, a country with a massive army but one made up largely of poorly trained and poorly equipped conscripts may have an equal or even a lesser number of FPs than a smaller but better-trained and better-equipped force.

Each faction will know how many Firepower Points it has; it will not possess this information about other factions, although it may learn it during the course of the game. This will likely occur because either an allied power has chosen to divulge its number of FPs or a careless player has leaked that information.

The mobilization plan (written as a paper, to be presented to the other members of the commander's faction) must contain the following:

1. A recommendation for when mobilization should take place. For example, a commander might call for mobilization to occur at once, immediately after some other power mobilizes, or when some other development arises. The recommendation should include a detailed justification, since it should be understood that while the commander is generally recognized as the faction's expert on military affairs, other faction members may be skeptical about his proposal.

2. A recommendation for how Firepower Points are to be deployed to each possible front (see table 1). For example, if a country has four FPs and borders three possible fronts, the commander must propose how the FPs will be allocated among the three. Here again the recommendation should include a detailed justification.

3. For each front where FPs are assigned, a recommendation as to whether the troops should be ordered to go on the offensive or to stand on the defensive.

4. Other elements as indicated in the commanders' individual role descriptions.

There are nine possible fronts on which combat may occur. Table 1 lists the possible fronts and which countries may commit FPs to the fronts. The fronts are depicted on the following page.

Once the members of a faction have agreed on the specific terms of the mobilization plan, the plan is submitted to the gamemaster. If no mobilization plan is agreed on, the country's armed forces will not be mobilized unless the country is attacked. (It should be noted that a country that must fight before it has mobilized its forces may only use half of its FPs; factions therefore have a considerable incentive to reach an agreement on how and when to mobilize.)

TABLE 1 The Fronts

	Front	May contain FPs owned by
1	Flanders*	Germany, France, Belgium, Great Britain
2	Lorraine	Germany, France
3	Alps	France, Italy
4	Dolomites	Italy, Austria-Hungary
5	Bohemia	Germany, Austria-Hungary (fighting here is theoretically possible but unlikely)
6	Poland	Germany, Russia
7	Galicia	Austria-Hungary, Russia, Romania
8	Balkans	Austria-Hungary, Serbia, Romania, Bulgaria, Greece
9	Caucasus	Russia, Ottoman Empire

*The first faction that mobilizes offensively on the Flanders front is assumed to have violated the neutrality of Belgium. This will result in Belgium joining the opposing side. Once Belgian neutrality has been violated, either side may subsequently mobilize offensively on the Flanders front without affecting Belgium's status.

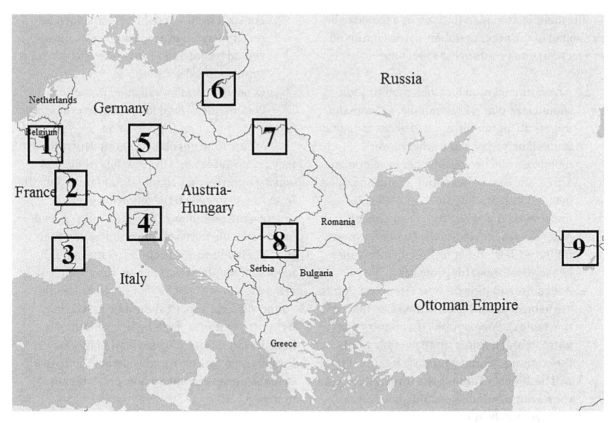

The Fronts

International Negotiations

Negotiations among the various countries represented in the game may happen at any time, either during class sessions (through passed notes or face-to-face conversation) or outside of class (through conversation, e-mails, instant messaging, etc.). Protocol normally dictates that discussion will occur between faction members who have the same essential function; for example, foreign ministers will communicate with other foreign ministers, military commanders with other military commanders (presumably of allied countries). Each role description includes a list of those individuals with whom a character may speak.

In 1914 there were two major alliance blocs: the Triple Alliance (Germany, Austria-Hungary, and Italy) and the Triple Entente (Great Britain, France, and Russia). It is not a requirement of the game that these alliances remain in place; members of each country's faction may negotiate with members of any other faction. Relations between the two blocs are tense, but there is no assumption that they will go to war against one another. At the same time, it would not be wise to assume that countries that are allied with one another have a unity of interests. Individual role descriptions will provide more information about how players should deal with members of other factions.

International Conferences

Ever since the end of the Napoleonic Wars, international conferences were the preferred methods for dealing with crises. Representatives of the great powers would gather in some location—usually a plush resort—to discuss difficult matters that might, if left unchecked, bring about war. These conferences would usually end with a treaty that all participants would sign.

Any foreign minister can propose an international conference to attempt to deal with the July Crisis. If one is proposed, each faction must decide (again, unanimously for most factions) whether it will participate. If two or more great powers (Britain, France, Germany, Austria-Hungary, Russia, and Italy [if in the game]) refuse to participate, the conference does not take place.

If an international conference is held, *it must take place during Game Session 2*. Each faction member of every participating country may be present to discuss the issue collectively. Anyone at the conference may propose a diplomatic solution to the crisis. The solution is then voted on by the representatives of the great powers (Britain, France, Germany, Italy [if in the game], Austria-Hungary, and Russia, with each faction receiving a single vote); other powers, if played, may send representatives to participate in the discussions, but they may not vote. A proposal is assumed to be approved if it receives a majority of votes, but any country may decide to defy the international community by refusing to accept a proposal that has been approved at a conference. Note that defying the decision of a conference is normally regarded as a serious breach of international etiquette. If a country suspects that a conference will not produce a favorable result, it is generally wiser to prevent the conference from happening in the first place.

Declarations of War and Neutrality

If the powers fail to reach a negotiated settlement of the July Crisis, international differences will be decided on the battlefield. No combat (see the following text) can take place between countries unless there has been a declaration of war. Any country may declare war on any other country at any point after the first game session, but a country cannot go to war for no reason. Your faction may declare war on another country in any of the following circumstances:

1. That country is Serbia, and you are part of the Austro-Hungarian faction.
2. That country declares war against a country with which you have an alliance.
3. That country mobilizes its armies in an area on your country's border and refuses to stand down upon being called upon to do so.
4. That country violates a treaty that your country has signed.
5. That country defies the decision of an international conference in which your country was a participant.
6. A member of that country's faction insults your country and refuses to apologize upon being called upon to do so (see Treitschke on the need for a state to possess "a very highly-developed sense of honor").

Decisions for war, like all other important decisions in the game, must be made unanimously within most factions. (As absolute monarchies, Germany and Russia may declare war even if one faction member opposes it, as long as the dissenting member isn't the kaiser or the tsar.) A country need not have completed the mobilization of its armed forces—or even started the process—before issuing a declaration of war. However, fighting may begin any time after war has been declared, and, as mentioned under "Mobilization," a country that is forced to fight before mobilization is complete may use only half of its FPs.

The drafting of a declaration of war is the responsibility of the faction's foreign minister. (Exception: in the French faction it is Poincaré—the president—who will have this responsibility; in this instance he is not actually declaring war, but asking the legislature to do so.) These declarations should be presented in the form of speeches during Game Session 2. Each declaration should include a detailed discussion of the events that led up to the decision to engage in hostilities and an explanation of why the country is justified in taking up arms. The audience for this declaration should be the other powers, particularly the neutrals, in the hope that they might eventually be drawn into the war as allies.

If, on the other hand, a faction does not agree to go to war, it is up to the foreign minister (or, in the case of France, the president) to draft a statement of neutrality (even if the foreign minister wanted war). This statement should explain why the country is remaining on the sidelines, and, if applicable, why it is justified in not going to war in defense of its allies (or in defense of other national interests). Again, the audience for this declaration should be the other powers.

Chief Executives and War

Once it has been determined whether or not a country will go to war, it is the job of each faction's chief executive (monarch or prime minister) to convey this to the country's citizens. (Exception: In the case of France, it is Viviani—who is both premiere and war minister—who has this responsibility.) This will take the form of a speech to the nation during Game Session 3. In some ways this speech will be similar to the foreign minister's declaration of war, in that it will seek to justify the decision. However, because the audience for this address will be domestic, it should attempt to persuade the public that the sacrifices that they can be expected to bear during the conflict are worthwhile. The speech should also touch on any special domestic circumstances that exist at the time (for example, Irish home rule for Great Britain; labor unrest in France, Germany, and Russia; ethnic tensions in Austria-Hungary), and explain why these must recede into the background for the duration of the conflict.

The gamemaster will judge the effectiveness of each chief executive's address. Those deemed particularly effective will produce an outpouring of patriotic fervor that will translate into bonuses on the battlefield. Those judged to be lackluster may result in reduced morale on the home front—a dangerous situation for any country at war.

Optional: Instructors who wish to encourage creative activity on the part of their students may invite them to prepare posters promoting service to the nation. For example, the students might design recruitment posters for the armed forces, or ones exhorting women to sacrifice on the home front. Particularly strong posters might affect morale. Another possibility would be for students to sing a stirring rendition of some patriotic song of the period (examples: "Deutschland über Alles," the "Marseillaise," or "Rule Britannia"). Again, effective performances might influence national morale.

Combat

At the end of Game Session 3, after the foreign ministers have issued their declarations of war or neutrality and the chief executives have addressed their nations, combat takes place. This will reflect the battles that take place in the first weeks of the war. In the normal three-session game, the results of this fighting will determine whether either side wins an outright victory and is able to bring its troops home "before the leaves fall," as the expression went.

If using the optional fourth session (see the following "Other Rules"), this initial round of fighting is not final, but it sets the stage for an additional round of negotiations in which those countries that remained neutral at the outset of the war may reconsider.

To resolve combat, the gamemaster reveals the mobilization plans of those countries that are at war. First, the number of Firepower Points that those countries have assigned to each front is made public. Fighting is assumed to take place on any front that borders any two powers that are at war with one another, as long as either power has committed at least one FP to it. For each front the number of FPs committed is revealed and compared with the others.

Second, one side must be designated the attacker, and the other the defender. This is done by revealing whether the mobilization plans of the powers involved call for the FPs in a front to go on the offensive or stand on the defensive. If both sides ordered their FPs to remain on the defensive, there is no combat. If one side designated its FPs for offense and the other designated its FPs for defense, then the former is the attacker, the latter the defender. If both sides' mobilization plans indicated that FPs on this front are to go on the offensive, the side that completed its mobilization first is considered the attacker.

Once the attacker is determined, odds are computed by dividing the number of FPs on that front owned by the attacker by the number of FPs controlled by the defender (rounding in favor of the defender). The attacker then rolls two dice and adds the results. Based on the die roll, the game-master determines which of the following outcomes occurs.

1. Major defeat. The attackers are routed, losing two FPs on that front.
2. Minor defeat. The attackers are driven back with heavy losses, losing one FP on that front.
3. Stalemate. No effect, with casualties on both sides.
4. Minor victory. The attackers advance, inflicting heavy casualties on the defenders, who lose one FP on that front.
5. Major victory: The defenders are routed, allowing the attackers to advance deep into enemy territory. The defenders lose two FPs on that front.

OBJECTIVES AND VICTORY CONDITIONS

Players win or lose in one of two ways.

1. *Faction victory* ("home before the leaves fall"): If a country goes to war and wins that war before the end of the final session, every member of that country's faction is assumed to win the game, as long as those members continue to hold their positions in government. Every player in every country that loses a war is assumed to lose. (Victory or defeat in a war is determined by number of victories and defeats on the various fronts, as well as the countries involved on each side.) If a country's government falls from office, every player in that faction loses, even if the country achieves a military victory.

2. *Individual victory*: If a country remains neutral, or if it has gone to war but has neither won nor lost, individual players win or lose based on the objectives stated in their role descriptions. Those who achieve 80 percent or more of their objectives are declared winners; those who achieve fewer than half lose.

Note that the first condition takes precedence over the second: a member of a faction that loses a war loses the game, even if he or she managed to achieve all of his or her individual objectives. The reverse is also true. This means that all players, no matter what their attitude to war was at the start of the game, have an interest in seeing their country win—or, at least, to avoid being defeated—once war is declared. In practice, this may mean agreeing to things that run contrary to their individual objectives, if those objectives seem likely to hinder the war effort.

OTHER RULES

Nonplayer Powers

In all games France, Germany, Austria-Hungary, and Russia are controlled by factions of players. If a sufficient number of players are available, additional countries may be involved: Great Britain (three players); Italy, the Ottoman Empire, Romania, and Greece (two players each); and Bulgaria and Serbia (one player each).

Any country that is not controlled by a faction of players is considered a nonplayer power. All nonplayer powers are assumed to remain neutral unless a player-controlled power declares war on them, or if they are "activated" by one side or the other. This may be done in the third or the optional fourth session; a die roll is made for each nonplayer power to see if it enters the war on either side.

There are various actions that can be taken by player-controlled powers to modify that die roll.

Belgium is always a nonplayer power, but may not be activated. It will remain neutral unless attacked.

Disputed Territories

Certain parts of Europe are disputed between countries, usually based on the ethnic makeup of their populations. These lands, and the countries disputing them, are listed in Table 2 below).

TABLE 2 Disputed Territories

	Territory	Owned by	Desired by
1	Alsace-Lorraine	Germany	France
2	Posen	Germany	Russia
3	East Prussia	Germany	Russia
4	Galicia	Austria-Hungary (Austrian half)	Russia
5	Trentino	Austria-Hungary (Austrian half)	Italy
6	Istria	Austria-Hungary (Austrian half)	Italy
7	Dalmatia	Austria-Hungary (Austrian half)	Italy and Serbia
8	Bosnia-Herzegovina	Austria-Hungary (Austrian half)	Serbia
9	Slavonia	Austria-Hungary (Hungarian half)	Serbia
10	Transylvania	Austria-Hungary (Hungarian half)	Romania
11	Bessarabia	Russia	Romania
12	Dobruja	Romania	Bulgaria
13	Skopje	Serbia	Bulgaria
14	Macedonia	Greece	Bulgaria
15	Thrace	Bulgaria	Greece
16	Edirne	Ottoman Empire	Bulgaria and Greece
17	Black Sea Straits	Ottoman Empire	Russia and Greece
18	Bursa	Ottoman Empire	Greece
19	Ionia	Ottoman Empire	Greece
20	Cyprus	Ottoman Empire	Greece
21	Crete	Greece	Ottoman Empire
22	Dodecanese Islands	Italy	Ottoman Empire and Greece
23	Batum-Kars	Russia	Ottoman Empire
24	Corsica	France	Italy
25	Nice	France	Italy
26	Savoy	France	Italy

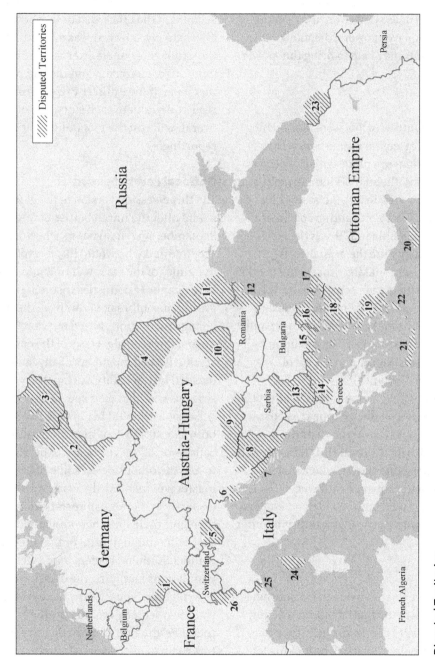

Disputed Territories

Certain characters in the game are instructed to seek written guarantees that these lands will be transferred to their countries, either peacefully (perhaps as a price for entering a war, or even for remaining neutral) or as spoils from a successful war. Offering a nonplayer power a disputed territory that it wants may help to bring that power into a war on your side.

Monarchs

Most European countries in 1914 were monarchies in which kings had at least some authority. However, only certain kings are represented by players in the game: Kaiser Wilhelm II of Germany and Tsar Nicholas II of Russia, and, in larger classes, King Carol I of Romania, King Constantine I of Greece, and Tsar Ferdinand of Bulgaria. This is because of all the monarchs, they were the most directly involved in the decision-making process during the July Crisis. Others either were constitutionally kept from a direct role (George V of England, for example) or made it clear from the outset that they would endorse any course that could be agreed upon by the leading statesmen (Kaiser Franz Josef of Austria-Hungary, for instance).

However, it is possible for monarchs to affect the deliberations even if they do not appear as characters, particularly if a player-monarch drafts a personal letter to his fellow royal. This letter should be submitted to the gamemaster, who will determine if the intended recipient is sufficiently influenced by it to send a message to the members of that faction encouraging war, neutrality, or other action.

Journalists

There may, in larger classes, be up to five journalists in the game. All come from the United States, trying to make sense of the events in Europe for their readers back home. They will be looking for interviews with the other players and should not be ignored. While there appears to be no chance that the Americans will abandon their traditional neutrality, it would be helpful for the European powers to have friends in the only great power unlikely to become involved in the looming conflict.

Each journalist has the job of producing an account of the crisis, discussing how war came or, alternatively, how war was averted. At the end of the game, the gamemaster and the other players (now out of character, and instead portraying members of the Pulitzer Prize committee) must read and evaluate each story. The one judged best overall will win the 1914 Pulitzer Prize for news reporting.

Optional Fourth Session

The three-session version of the game is designed to end after the initial battles of August–September 1914. Instructors who are able to spare the time and who would like to explore more of the dynamics of the early war may add a fourth session in which those countries that remained neutral during the outbreak of war have the opportunity to change their minds based on what happened during the opening weeks of the conflict. If a fourth session is used, members of any faction that decided on neutrality during the second and third sessions will give their speeches during session 4.

Session 4 should begin with negotiations, as both sides try to convince the neutrals to join their cause—or, at the very least, to persuade them not to join the other side. At some point the gamemaster will then ask if any neutrals would like to declare war. Foreign ministers from those powers then give their speeches, announcing either that they will remain neutral or that they will enter the conflict. National leaders may then address their populations justifying the decision either to fight or to remain at peace. Any factions that enter the war must secretly record how they are allocating their FPs and indicate whether they are committing them to offense or defense.

After the neutrals are finished, the original belligerents have an opportunity to shift FPs from one front to another, and decide whether they will be used for offense or defense. This should also be recorded secretly. Once this step is complete, all sides will reveal how they have allocated their FPs, and a second round of combat is resolved in each front containing FPs belonging to a country at war. Afterward, the numbers of victories and defeats, as well as the countries arrayed on both sides, are totaled to determine whether the war has ended.

BASIC OUTLINE OF THE GAME

The game itself is played over the course of three class sessions, with the option of a fourth. First, even before the first session the members of the Austro-Hungarian faction must meet to decide on a response to the assassination of Franz Ferdinand; once reached, that decision is conveyed to the other players. If a response is needed from Serbia, the Russian faction will determine what it will be. (In larger classes Serbia may be represented by a "faction" of a single player, who will make this decision.)

During the first session, the members of most factions must agree as to what the circumstances must be for the country to mobilize the armed forces. Should it happen automatically on a particular date? Or should it be carried out in response to something that another country does? In this session it is either the war minister or army chief of staff who will do most of the talking, presenting the country's military plans and putting forward his views on when mobilization must occur, and against whom. (The British faction, which does not have a war minister or chief of staff, will have a somewhat different goal for the first session.) Before the end of this session, each faction must complete and submit a Mobilization Form that informs the gamemaster (privately) what was agreed upon. If members of a faction fail to agree, it is assumed that mobilization will not take place unless another country declares war on it.

Based on the mobilization plans developed during the first sessions, the gamemaster then announces which countries have mobilized against one another, and in what order—although the precise allocation of Firepower Points (FPs)

will remain secret. There will likely be a flurry of diplomatic activity at this point, and perhaps an attempt at international mediation of the crisis. Armed with this information, the foreign ministers of each faction then come to the second session prepared to make a speech, either declaring war or announcing neutrality. (Often it will be unclear until the second session whether or not a country will go to war; in these cases, foreign ministers should come prepared to declare *either* war or neutrality.) Diplomatic wrangling, final decisions for war (which, again, must be made unanimously within most factions, or with the consent of the monarch and one other faction member in the case of Germany and Russia) and the foreign ministers' speeches will occupy the second session.

During the third session one member of each faction (normally the head of state—president, prime minister, kaiser, tsar, etc.) makes a public address to his people, explaining either why they are being called upon to make the great sacrifices entailed by war or why the country must remain at peace. At the end of this session the gamemaster will reveal the allocation of FPs to the various fronts, and the initial battles of the war are resolved by die roll. The goal for all belligerents is to win and bring home their troops "before the leaves fall."

Assuming that neither side wins a decisive victory at the outset, instructors may opt for a fourth game session, representing the situation in autumn 1914. Based on how the war has gone so far (i.e., the results of the die rolls made at the end of session 3), and the no-doubt-feverish diplomatic efforts of the belligerent countries since then, any countries that remained neutral at the start of the war have the option of entering. If this optional fourth session is used, foreign ministers and national leaders of powers that remained neutral in session 3 postpone their speeches until this one. The attitude of states that are not represented by players in the game will be determined by die roll. At the end of this session another round of die rolls will decide whether the war ends before the end of the year.

ASSIGNMENTS

Each player will generally be expected to write one paper and to give one speech based on that paper. The military commander's job is to develop a mobilization plan and present it to the other members of his faction. The foreign minister is responsible for drafting a declaration of war or of neutrality and presenting that to members of all factions (in other words, to the entire class). The chief executive is tasked with writing and giving an address to the people of his nation (although, in practice, it will be to the class).

Optionally, instructors may require that each player create a poster designed to exhort his or her country's citizenry to sacrifice for the good of the nation. This might be a call to enlist in the armed forces, to buy war bonds, or to conserve food or other resources. A good source of inspiration for such posters is http://www.ww1propaganda.com/.

4

Roles and Factions

AUSTRIA-HUNGARY

Count Leopold Berchtold: Foreign minister of Austria-Hungary since 1912; one of the wealthiest men in Central Europe; reputed to be a cautious moderate but determined to prevent Serbian expansion; known to have been close to the murdered Archduke Franz Ferdinand.

General Franz Conrad von Hötzendorf: Chief of staff of the Austro-Hungarian Army and Navy since 1906 (aside from a brief interlude in 1911–12); a military hothead who has repeatedly called for war against Serbia and who will certainly do so again in this instance.

István Tisza: Prime minister of Hungary since 1913; defender of the Dual Monarchy but dedicated to preserving Magyar supremacy over Hungary; a determined opponent of Franz Ferdinand's proposed reforms.

FRANCE

Raymond Poincaré: President of France since 1913; conservative, a native of Lorraine, an implacable enemy of Germany and passionate supporter of the Franco-Russian Alliance.

René Viviani: Prime minister of France and minister of foreign affairs for just over two weeks at the time of Franz Ferdinand's assassination; a socialist who bucked the party line by supporting increased military spending and a law requiring that all Frenchmen perform a minimum of three years of military service; nevertheless, reputed to be antiwar and skeptical of France's alliance with Russia.

General Joseph Jacque Césaire Joffre: Commander-in-chief of the French Army since 1911 but disliked by the present left-wing government for his conservative views; experienced mainly in military engineering and logistics but a great believer in the "cult of the offensive."

GERMANY

Kaiser Wilhelm II: Emperor of Germany since 1888; believer in absolute monarchy; cousin of King George V of Great Britain and Tsar Nicholas II of

Russia; a lover of military uniforms and warships and prone to sweeping warlike pronouncements but rumored to be secretly terrified by the prospect of war.

Theobald von Bethmann-Hollweg: Chancellor of Germany since 1909; tireless advocate of improved relations with Great Britain; regarded as a moderate in both domestic and foreign affairs.

General Helmuth von Moltke: Chief of the German General Staff since 1906; commonly referred to as "Moltke the Younger" to distinguish him from his uncle of the same name who held the same position from 1871 to 1888; advocate of war to liberate Germany from its "encirclement" by Britain, France, and Russia.

GREAT BRITAIN

Herbert H. Asquith: Prime minister of Great Britain since 1908; leader of the Liberal Party; preoccupied with the situation in Ireland with comparatively little interest in foreign affairs.

Sir Edward Grey: British foreign secretary since 1905; known Liberal imperialist; champion of the Anglo-French Entente; believer in the balance of power.

David Lloyd George: British chancellor of the exchequer since 1908; leader of the radical faction within the Liberal Party; opposed to imperialism and war; believed to be sympathetic to Germany and hostile toward Russia.

RUSSIA

Tsar Nicholas II: Emperor and autocrat of all the Russias since 1892; torn between support for pan-Slavism and fear of what war might do to Russia; cousin of Kaiser Wilhelm II.

Sergei Dmitrievich Sazonov: Foreign minister of Russia since 1910; pro-French, often criticized by nationalists for insufficiently championing the pan-Slav idea; worried about German ambitions in the Ottoman Empire.

General Vladimir Aleksandrovich Sukhomlinov: War minister of Russia since 1909; personally close to Tsar Nicholas; a passionate advocate of the

offensive who ordered reallocation of resources away from static fortifications and toward infantry and mobile artillery.

ITALY

Antonio Salandra: Prime minister of Italy since March 1914; an authoritarian conservative from a wealthy middle-class family; a former professor dedicated to territorial expansion.

Antonino Paternò-Castello, marchese di San Giuliano: Foreign minister of Italy since 1910; scion of a noble family from Sicily; has sought to cultivate close relations with Germany while trying to limit Austrian gains in the Balkans.

OTTOMAN EMPIRE

Ahmed Djemal Pasha: Turkish minister of the navy since February 1914; rumored to be pro-British but deeply distrustful of Russia.

Ismail Enver Pasha: Turkish minister of war since February 1914; formerly military attaché to Berlin; believed to desire an alliance with Germany.

BULGARIA

Ferdinand I: Tsar of Bulgaria since 1908; highly ambitious; regarded as thoroughly unscrupulous; seeks revenge against Serbia for Bulgaria's losses in the Second Balkan War.

SERBIA

Nikola Pašić: Prime minister of Serbia since 1903 (with the exception of a few months in 1908); believed to be a moderate nationalist but under intense pressure from officers of the Serbian Army; perhaps too inclined to tolerate anti-Austrian activities on Serbian soil.

ROMANIA

Carol I: King of Romania since 1866; a member of a branch of the Hohenzollern family; inclined to be pro-German; seeks the return of Bessarabia, taken by Russia after the Russo-Turkish War of 1877–78.

Ion Bratianu: Eleven-time prime minister and the single most powerful politician in Romania;

known to be pro-French and to desire better relations with Russia; seeks to annex Transylvania, a province of the Austro-Hungarian Empire inhabited primarily by Romanians.

GREECE

Constantine I: King of Greece since 1913; brother-in-law of Kaiser Wilhelm II of Germany and therefore believed to harbor pro-German sympathies. As a young monarch he is eager to make his mark on the country and may be tempted to go to war in pursuit of territorial gains.

Eleutherios Venizelos: Prime minister since 1909 and likely the most powerful politician in Greece. A passionate advocate of territorial expansion, he is looking for opportunities to take land from Bulgaria and the Ottoman Empire and likely to work with whichever side is prepared to help him achieve that goal.

JOURNALISTS

These aren't exactly a faction, since each journalist is competing against all of the others. However, they do not fit neatly into any of the other categories. All are from the United States, seeking to explain developments in Europe to their readers back home.

Richard Harding Davis: Probably the world's best-known war correspondent; originally came to fame for his coverage of the Spanish-American War; also, author of thirty-five books.

Mary Boyle O'Reilly: Daughter of the Irish revolutionary John Boyle O'Reilly; a progressive reformer and "muckraker" who now serves as London correspondent for the Newspaper Enterprise Association.

William Henry Irwin: A well-known muckraking journalist who is trying his hand at international coverage for the first time.

Mary Roberts Rinehart: A novelist, known for mysteries and comedies, now serving as foreign correspondent for the *Saturday Evening Post*.

Frederick Palmer: Well-known war correspondent who has covered nearly every international conflict since the Greco-Turkish War.

5

Core Texts

VATTEL

EXCERPT FROM EMER DE VATTEL,
THE LAW OF NATIONS (1758)

Emer de Vattel (1714–67) was a prominent Swiss scholar of international law. His The Law of Nations, *originally published in 1758, portrayed the law as an evolving standard based on actual practice rather than as an idealistic formulation of how nations ought to behave. Vattel's work was highly influential in the late eighteenth and nineteenth centuries, and was published in multiple editions.*

§47. *Political equilibrium.* Europe forms a political system, an integral body, closely connected by the relations and different interests of the nations inhabiting this part of the world. It is not, as formerly, a confused heap of detached pieces, each of which thought herself very little concerned in the fate of the others, and seldom regarded things which did not immediately concern her. The continual attention of sovereigns to every occurrence, the constant residence of ministers, and the perpetual negotiations, make of modern Europe a kind of republic, of which the members—each independent, but all linked together by the ties of common interest—unite for the maintenance of order and liberty. Hence arose that famous scheme of the political balance, or the equilibrium of power; by which is understood such a disposition of things, as that no one potentate be able absolutely to predominate, and prescribe laws to the others.

§48. *Ways of maintaining it.* The surest means of preserving that equilibrium would be, that no power should be much superior to the others,—that all, or at least the greater part, should be nearly equal in force. Such a project has been attributed to Henry the Fourth [King of France, 1589–1610]: but it would have been impossible to carry it into execution without injustice and violence. Besides, suppose such equality once established, how could it always be maintained by lawful means? Commerce, industry, military pre-eminence, would soon put an end to it. The right of inheritance, vesting even in women and their descendents,—a rule, which it was so absurd to establish in the case of sovereignties, but which nevertheless is established,—would completely overturn the whole system.

It is a more simple, an easier, and a more equitable plan, to have recourse to the method just mentioned, of forming confederacies in order to oppose the more powerful potentate, and prevent him from giving law to his neighbors. Such is the mode at present pursued by the sovereigns of Europe. They consider the two principal powers, which on that very account are naturally rivals, as destined to be checks on each other; and they unite with the weaker, like so many weights thrown into the lighter scale, in order to keep it in equilibrium with the other. The house of Austria has long been the preponderating power: at present France is so in her turn. England, whose opulence and formidable fleets have a powerful influence, without alarming any state on the score of its liberty, because that nation seems cured of the rage of conquest,—England, I say, has the glory of holding the political balance. She is attentive to preserve it in equilibrium:—a system of policy, which is in itself highly just and wise, and will ever entitle her to praise, as long as she continues to pursue it only by means of alliances, confederacies, and other methods equally lawful.

§49. How he who destroys the equilibrium may be restrained, or even weakened. Confederacies would be a sure mode of preserving the equilibrium, and thus maintaining the liberty of nations, did all princes thoroughly understand their true interests, and make the welfare of the state serve as the rule in all their proceedings. Great potentates, however, are but too successful in gaining over partisans and allies, who blindly adopt all their views. Dazzled by the glare of a present advantage, seduced by their avarice, deceived by faithless ministers,—how many princes become the tools of a power which will one day swallow up either themselves or their successors! The safest plan, therefore, is to seize the first favorable opportunity when we can, consistently with

justice, weaken that potentate who destroys the equilibrium—or to employ every honorable means to prevent his acquiring too formidable a degree of power. For that purpose, all the other nations should be particularly attentive not to suffer him to aggrandize himself by arms: and this they may at all times do with justice. For if this prince makes an unjust war, every one has a right to succor the oppressed party. If he makes a just war, the neutral nations may interfere as mediators for an accommodation,—they may induce the weaker state to propose reasonable terms and offer a fair satisfaction,—and may save her from falling under the yoke of a conqueror. On the offer of equitable conditions to the prince who wages even the most justifiable war, he has all that he can demand. The justice of his cause, as we shall soon see, never gives him a right to subjugate his enemy, unless when that extremity becomes necessary to his own safety, or when he has no other mode of obtaining indemnification for the injury he has received. Now, that is not the case here, as the interposing nations can by other means procure him a just indemnification, and an assurance of safety.

In fine, there cannot exist a doubt, that, if that formidable potentate certainly entertain designs of oppression and conquest,—if he betray his views by his preparations and other proceedings,—the other states have a right to anticipate him: and if the fate of war declares in their favour, they are justifiable in taking advantage of this happy opportunity to weaken and reduce a power too contrary to the equilibrium, and dangerous to the common liberty.

Source: Emer de Vattel, The Law of Nations; or, Principles of the Law of Nature, applied to the Conduct and Affairs of Nations and Sovereigns. From the French of Monsieur de Vattel. *From the New Edition by Joseph Chitty, with additional notes and references by Edward D. Ingraham (Philadelphia: T. & J. W. Johnson, 1883), http://oll.libertyfund .org/titles/2245; accessed July 21, 2015.*

COBDEN
- Merchant and factory owner in England
- Free trade to build peace

EXCERPT FROM RICHARD COBDEN, "THE BALANCE OF POWER" (1835)

Richard Cobden (1804–1865) was a successful merchant and factory owner in Manchester, England. His travels abroad convinced him that free trade could bring about a more peaceful and prosperous world, and this led him to become involved in politics. In 1838 he cofounded the Anti–Corn Law League, an organization seeking the repeal of high tariffs against imported grain. He was elected to Parliament in 1841, where he finally achieved the repeal of the Corn Laws five years later. Cobden also advocated a noninterventionist foreign policy and denounced Britain's involvement in the Crimean War and the Opium Wars. In this, one of his earlier speeches, he dismisses the balance of power as a "chimera" useful only as a pretext for war.

Our history during the last century may be called the tragedy of "British intervention in the politics of Europe;" in which princes, diplomatists, peers, and generals have been the authors and actors—the people the victims; and the moral will be exhibited to the latest posterity in 800 millions of debt.

We have said that our proposal to reduce our armaments will be opposed upon the plea of maintaining a proper attitude, as it is called, amongst the nations of Europe. British intervention in the state policy of the Continent has been usually excused under the two stock pretences of maintaining the balance of power in Europe, and of protecting our commerce; upon which two subjects, as they bear indirectly on the question in hand, we shall next offer a few observations.

The first instance in which we find the "balance of power" alluded to in a king's speech is on the occasion of the last address of William III. to his Parliament, December 31, 1701, where he concludes by saying—"I will only add this—if you do in good earnest desire to see England hold the balance of Europe, it will appear by your right improving the present opportunity." From this period down to almost our time (latterly indeed, the phrase has become, like many other cant terms, nearly obsolete), there will be found, in almost every successive king's speech, a constant recurrence to the "balance of Europe;" by which, we may rest assured, war always means, however it might be concealed under pretended alarm for the "equilibrium of power" or the "safety of the Continent," the desire to see England "hold the balance." The phrase was found to please the public ear; it implied something of equity; whilst England, holding the balance of Europe in her hand, sounded like filling the office of Justice herself to one half of the globe. Of course such a post of honour could not be maintained, or its dignity asserted, without a proper attendance of guards and officers, and we consequently find that at about this period of our history large standing armies began to be called for; and not only were the supplies solicited by the government from time to time under the plea of preserving the liberties of Europe, but in the annual mutiny bill (the same in form as is now passed every year) the preamble stated, amongst other motives, that the annual army was voted for the purpose of preserving the balance of power in Europe. The "balance of power," then, becomes an important practical subject for investigation. It appeals directly to the business and bosoms of our readers, since it is implicated with an expenditure of more than a dozen millions of money per annum, every farthing of which goes, in the shape of taxation, from the pockets of the public.

Such of our readers as have not investigated this subject will not be a little astonished to find a great discrepancy in the several definitions of what is actually meant by the "balance of power." The theory—for it has never yet been applied to practice—appears, after upwards of a century of acknowledged existence, to be less understood now than ever. Latterly, indeed, many intelligent and practical-minded politicians have thrown the question overboard, along with that of the balance of trade, of which number, without participating in their favoured attributes, we claim to be ranked as one. The balance of power, which has for a hundred years been the burden of kings' speeches, the theme of statesmen, the ground of solemn treaties, and the cause of wars; which has served, down to the very year in which we write, and which will, no doubt, continue to serve for years to come as a pretence for maintaining enormous standing armaments by land and sea, at a cost of many hundreds of millions of treasure—the balance of power is a chimera! It is not a fallacy, a mistake, an imposture, it is an undescribed, indescribable, incomprehensible nothing; mere words, conveying to the mind not ideas, but sounds like those equally barren syllables which our ancestors put together for the purpose of puzzling themselves about words. . . .

Critique with examples

. . . At what epoch did the nations of the Continent subscribe to that constitution "by virtue of which," according to Gentz, "no one among them can injure the independence or essential rights of another?" Did this constitution exist whilst Britain was spoiling the Dutch at the Cape or in the east? or when she dispossessed France of Canada? or (worse outrage by far) did it exist when England violated the "essential rights" of Spain by taking forcible and felonious possession of a portion of her native soil? Had this constitution been subscribed by Russia, Prussia, and Austria at the moment when they signed the partition of Poland? or by France when she amalgamated with a portion of Switzerland? By Austria at the acquisition of Lombardy? by Russia when dismembering Sweden, Turkey, and Persia? or by Prussia before incorporating Silesia?

So far from any such confederation having ever been, by written, verbal, or implied agreement, entered into by the "European powers, obeying certain laws, and actuated in general by a common principle;" the theory of the balance of power has, we believe, generally been interpreted, by those who, from age to age, have, parrotlike, used the phrase, to be a system invented for the very purpose of supplying the want of such a combination. Regarding it for a moment in this point of view, we should still expect to find that the

"balancing system" had, at some period of modern history, been recognised and agreed to by all the Continental states; and that it had created a spirit of mutual concession and guarantee, by which the weaker and more powerful empires were placed upon a footing of equal security, and by which any one potentate or state was absolutely unable "to predominate over the others." But, instead of any such self-denial, we discover that the balance of Europe has merely meant (if it has had a meaning) that which our blunt Dutch king openly avowed as his aim to his parliament—a desire, on the part of the great powers, to "hold the balance of Europe." England has, for nearly a century, held the European scales—not with the blindness of the goddess of justice herself, or with a view to the equilibrium of opposite interests, but with a Cyclopean eye to her own aggrandisement. The same lust of conquest has actuated, up to the measure of their abilities, the other great powers; and, if we find the smaller states still, in the majority of instances, preserving their independent existence, it is owing, not to the watchful guardianship of the "balancing system," but to the limits which nature herself has set to the undue extension of territorial dominion—not only by the physical boundaries of different countries, but in those still more formidable moral impediments to the invader—the unity of language, laws, customs, and traditions; the instinct of patriotism and freedom; the hereditary rights of rulers; and, though last not least, that homage to the restraints of justice which nations and public bodies have in all ages avowed, however they may have found excuses for evading it.

So far, then, as we can understand the subject, the theory of a balance of power is a mere chimera—a creation of the politician's brain—a phantasm, without definite form or tangible existence—a mere conjunction of syllables, forming words which convey sound without meaning. Yet these words have been echoed by the greatest orators and statesmen of England . . . ay, even whilst we were in the act of stripping the maritime nations of the Continent of their colonies, then regarded as the sole source of commercial greatness; whilst we stood sword in hand upon the neck of Spain, or planted our standard on the rock of Malta; and even when England usurped the dominion of the ocean, and attempted to extend the sphere of human despotism over another element, by insolently putting barriers upon that highway of nations—even then the tongues of our orators resounded most loudly with the praises of the "balance of power!" There would be something peculiarly humiliating in connection with this subject, in beholding the greatest minds of successive ages, instead of exercising the faculty of thought, become the mere automata of authority, and retail, with less examination than the haberdasher bestows upon the length, breadth, and quality of his wares, the sentiments bequeathed from former generations of writers and speakers—but that, unhappily, the annals of philosophy and of past religions afford too many examples of the triumph of mere imitativeness over the higher faculties of the human intellect. . . .

The balance of power, then, might in the first place, be very well dismissed as chimera, because no state of things, such as the "disposition," "constitution," or "union" of European powers referred to as the basis of their system, by Vattel,[1] Gentz,[2] and Brougham,[3] ever did exist; and, secondly, the theory could, on other grounds, be discarded as fallacious, since it gives no definition—whether by breadth of territory, number of inhabitants, or extent of wealth— according to which, in balancing the respective

1. Emer de Vattel (1714–67) was a Swiss scholar who in 1758 published *The Law of Nations*.

2. Friedrich von Gentz (1764–1832) was a Prussian diplomat who in 1806 published *Fragments upon the Balance of Power in Europe*.

3. Henry Brougham, 1st Baron Brougham and Vaux (1778–1868), was a British statesman of the early- to mid-nineteenth century. An advocate of free trade and passionate enemy of the slave trade, Brougham was Lord High Chancellor of Great Britain from 1830 to 1834.

powers, each state shall be estimated; whilst, lastly, it would be altogether incomplete and inoperative from neglecting, or refusing to provide against, the silent and peaceful aggrandisements which spring from improvement and labour. . . .

Source: Richard Cobden, The Political Writings of Richard Cobden, *F. W. Chesson, ed. London: T. Fisher Unwin, 1903, Library of Economics and Liberty, http://www.econlib.org/library/ YPDBooks /Cobden/cbdPW6.html, accessed July 21, 2015.*

TIMES OF LONDON
"THE BULWARK OF PEACE" (1914)

On April 8, 1914, the Times *of London ran this editorial, praising the balance of power for having safeguarded the peace of Europe despite numerous international crises. The article was carried by many other newspapers throughout Europe in the days and weeks to follow.*

It is ten years to-day since the signature of the Agreements which embody the Entente between England and France. They have been momentous years. They have witnessed immense changes, and changes fraught with the utmost peril to peace. The war between Japan and Russia, the collapse of two great monarchies in Asia, and revolution in a third, the downfall of Morocco as a sovereign State, and the creation of the French protectorate, the conclusion of the Anglo-Russian agreement, the incorporation of Bosnia-Herzegovina in the Dual Monarchy, the African conquests of Italy, and the wars of the Balkan allies against Turkey and amongst themselves, have been amongst the events which they have seen. Anxious care, mutual suspicions, and at certain moments, acute alarm, have filled the Cabinets of Europe, while they have passed away. All these transformations, great in themselves, and pregnant with yet greater consequences, have been accomplished, and no Great Power has drawn the sword against another. That, we are firmly convinced, has been due, in the first place, to the great act of reconciliation we commemorate to-day. It was not a mere piece of statecraft. It was more than a sagacious arrangement for the accommodation of old controversies and the promotion of common interests. It was accepted by two great nations, frankly and without reserve, as the basis and as the consecration of a firm and abiding friendship. That is the vital principle of the Entente. That has made it thrive and grow with the years. That has enabled it to withstand all strains from within and from without. That leaves it deep-rooted to-day, with the promise of fresh growth and fresh developments to come. For ten troubled years it has stood the test. It has been exposed to many searching ordeals. Open assault and furtive sap, brutal menace and subtle intrigue have not been spared against it. All has been in vain. The Entente, expanded and supplemented by the Anglo-Russian Agreement, remains the bedrock of its members' whole international policy and an essential bulwark of the world's peace.

The Anglo-French agreement had not been signed a year when the first efforts were made to destroy it. Scarce had the news of Russia's final defeat at Mukden[4] reached Europe, when the German Emperor hurried to Tangier to make ostentatious proffers of protection to Morocco.[5] Russia, for whose Asiatic adventure Germany had had nothing but encouragement and praise, was manifestly unable to give her French ally effectual support. From complaisance for her pacifists France herself had neglected her means of defence. What better moment could there be to punish her audacity in having a foreign policy of her own, and to demonstrate the impotence of her allies and of her friends to save her from the wrath of Prussia-Germany? We need not dwell here upon the history of the campaign that followed. Prince Bülow, who

had declared a few months before that the Entente did not hurt German interests, now discovered that France had insulted Germany by neglecting to supplement the communication of the arrangement which she had made to the German Ambassador before it was signed by an official notification after it had been signed. The whole German Press was mobilized to threaten France, and all the strength of German diplomacy was exerted to ensure the sacrifice of the statesman who had triumphantly shattered the cherished tradition of the *Wilhelmstrasse*[6] that friendship between France and England was inconceivable. The sacrifice was made. The Radical capitalists threw over M. Delcassé.[7] Germany had her will, and forced France to assent to the Algeciras Conference. But there she learnt what the Entente means, and there she brought that lesson home to France, as no parchments and no protestations on our part could have done. When the Conference was over the whole world realized that we were ready to support by all means at our command the reasonable and legitimate claims of France, and in particular her claim to treat, and be treated by, every Great Power in all respects an equal. We had vindicated once again the continuous tradition of our national life, which rejects and resists pretensions from any quarter to the hegemony of Europe. The bonds of the Entente were drawn closer than before, and the way prepared for its necessary and logical completion by the conclusion two years later of our Agreement with Russia.

From that time forward the Triple Alliance has found its counterpoise in the balance of power. It is the equilibrium thus established which enabled France to emerge unhumiliated from the dubious

---

4. Fought in Manchuria in February–March 1906, the Battle of Mukden was the largest and most decisive land engagement of the Russo-Japanese War.

5. The kaiser's visit sparked the First Moroccan Crisis (see narrative).

6. The German Foreign Ministry, so named for the street in Berlin on which its offices were located.

7. Théophile Delcassé was the French foreign minister who negotiated the Anglo-French Entente. German pressure on France during the Morocco crisis brought about his resignation in 1906.

intrigues into which she was lured during the Monis and Caillaux Ministries,[8] and to sustain with tranquil dignity the challenge of Agadir. It is this which has made it possible for other powers to see the formidable question of the Near East opened in Bosnia-Herzegovina, in Tripoli, and in the Balkans without rushing to arms. It is this which led them during the most acute periods of the prolonged crisis in that peninsula to discuss their conflicting interests and desires with restraint and moderation through their Ambassadors in London. It is this which leaves their relations in all cases correct, and in almost all cases friendly, to-day. It is this which affords the world its best hopes of peace in the future. The division of the Great Powers into two well-balanced groups with intimate relations between the members of each, which do not forbid any such member from being on the friendliest terms with one or two members of the other, is a twofold check upon the inordinate ambitions or sudden outbursts of race hatred. All Sovereigns and statesmen—aye, and all nations—know that a war of group against group would be a measureless calamity. That knowledge brings with it a sense of responsibility which chastens and restrains the boldest and the most reckless. But they know, too, that to secure the support of the other members of their own group and to induce them to share the responsibility and the risks of such a conflict, any Power or Powers which may meditate recourse to arms must first satisfy these other members that the quarrel is necessary and just. They are no longer unfettered judges in their own case, answerable to none but to themselves. That the Triple Entente bears the character we have

ascribed to it, and has been for some years one of the twin pillars on which the peace of Europe and of Asia rests, is proved by the facts we have recounted. It is proved as well by the recorded statements made on behalf of Germany and of Russia. After the Björkö meeting[9] of the two Emperors in 1909 it was officially declared that the international arrangements to which those countries were parties were in no way opposed to the good relations between them, while an inspired newspaper remarked that "in the recent difficult times" the grouping of the Powers "had thoroughly stood the test." Still more explicit and significant is the communiqué issued after the Port Baltic meeting[10] of the same potentates in 1912. Then it was proclaimed that both new agreements and alterations of any kind in the grouping of the European Powers were out of the question. "The value of that grouping," it was added, "for the maintenance of equilibrium and of peace has already been proved." It has been proved continuously and yet more clearly in the vicissitudes which have occurred since those words were written. The balance of power is now the cardinal factor in the policy of the Old World. We owe it and all the developments it may bring to the Entente which is ten years old to-day.

Source: "The Bulwark of Peace," Times of London, *April 8, 1914, 14.*

8. Ernest Monis and Joseph Caillaux were successive prime ministers of France in 1911–12. Both men, in contrast with their predecessors, sought better relations with Germany. Caillaux was forced to resign after it was revealed that he had entered into negotiations with Berlin without having first informed Armand Fallières, the president of France at the time.

9. In July 1905 Kaiser Wilhelm II and Tsar Nicholas II met on the island of Björkö, just off Russia's Baltic coast. There they signed a defensive alliance, promising mutual aid if either were attacked. Neither monarch, however, had consulted with his government before doing so, and Russia's prime minister and foreign minister pointed out that the treaty violated the country's previously made commitment to France. Therefore, it was never ratified.

10. The tsar and the kaiser met again in July 1912, this time at Port Baltic, accompanied by their foreign ministers. While no treaty was signed, the two monarchs announced that relations between Russia and Germany were "harmonious."

German historian, nationalist, political theorist

VON TREITSCHKE

EXCERPTS FROM HEINRICH VON TREITSCHKE, *POLITICS* (1897–98)

Heinrich von Treitschke (1834–96) was a distinguished German historian and political theorist. He also served in the Reichstag, where he was an unapologetic supporter of monarchism as well as a fervent German nationalist. Politics was a collection of his lectures assembled by his students at the University of Berlin after his death. The selections that follow deal with international law, which he argues can never be laid down as a set of hard-and-fast rules. Ultimately, Treitschke believes that national interest must trump all other considerations.

It is essential . . . to go to work historically, and to consider the State as what it is as physical force, though at the same time as an institution intended to assist the education of the human race. In so far as it is physical force, the State will have a natural inclination to snatch for itself such earthly possessions as it desires for its own advantage. It is by its very nature grasping. Every State will, however, of its own accord, show a certain consideration for neighboring States. As a result of reasoned calculation, as well as from a mutual sense of their own advantage, the States will exhibit an increasing respect for justice. The State comes to realize that it is bound up with the common life of the States among which it is situated. Every State will, as a matter of course, observe certain restraints in its dealings with neighboring States. From reasoned calculation, from a reciprocal recognition of self-interest, a more definite sense of justice will develop with the course of time. The formal part of International Law for instance, the theory of the inviolability of ambassadors, with all its accompanying ceremonial developed comparatively early and securely. In modern Europe the privileges of Ambassadors, with all that this entails, are absolutely secure. It is safe to say that the formal side of International Law is much more firmly established and is much less frequently transgressed than are the rules of municipal justice in most States. Nevertheless, since there is placed above the States

no higher power which can decide between them, the existence of International Law is always precarious. It always must remain a *lex imperfecta.*[11] Everything depends upon reciprocity; and, since there is no supreme authority capable of exercising compulsion, the influence of science, and, above all, of public opinion, will play an important part. Savigny[12] declared International Law to be . . . a law in constant process of evolution. This, however, by no means implies that International Law is void of meaning. This evolving law has indeed a palpable effectiveness, the consequences of which we can trace in their developments up to the present day. There can be no doubt that the development of modern International Law was very materially influenced by Christianity. Christianity created a spirit of cosmopolitanism, in the noblest sense of the word; and it was therefore only reasonable and logical that, for centuries, the Porte[13] should not have come within the province of European International Law. The Porte was not in a position to profit fully by the benefits of European International Law, so long as it was exclusively swayed by Mohammedan[14] ideas of morality. It is only in recent times, since Christianity has become so strong in the Balkan Peninsula as to thrust Mohammedanism comparatively into the background, that the Porte has been invited to participate in international negotiations.

History shows us that great States are continually developing out of small States which have outlived their vitality. The great States must finally attain such a measure of power that they can stand on their own feet, that they are self-sufficing. Such a State must desire that peace should be main-

11. "Imperfect law."

12. Friedrich Carl von Savigny (1779–1861) was a well-known legal scholar who headed Prussia's judicial system in the 1850s.

13. The government of the Ottoman Empire was often referred to as "the Sublime Porte."

14. That is, Islamic.

tained, for the sake of its existence and for that of the treasures of civilization which it has under its care. So, out of this common sense of justice, there ensues an organized society of States, a so-called political system. Such a system is, however, impossible, apart from a certain at least approximate equilibrium between the Powers. The idea of a balance of power in Europe was at first, as we have seen, conceived very literally; but it does contain a germ of truth. We must not think of it as a *trutina gentium*,[15] with both scales on the same level; but an organized political system presupposes that no one State shall be so powerful as to be able to do just as it pleases without danger to itself. Here we see very clearly the superiority of the European system over the crude state-system of America. In America the United States can do just as they please. It is only because their ties with the small South American Republics are still very slight that the latter have not yet suffered any direct interference on the part of their great neighbor.

. . . It is very unfortunate for the science of International Law that countries like Belgium and Holland should so long have been its home. These countries, because they are in constant fear of being attacked, take a sentimental view of the subject, and tend to make claims on the victor in the name of humanity, claims which are unnatural and unreasonable and contrary to the power of the State. The treaties of Nijmegen and Ryswick[16] remind us that, in the seventeenth century, Holland was looked upon as the proper scene for the drama of *la haute politique*.[17] Switzerland, at a later date, enjoyed the same reputation. And, at the present day, few people trouble to think how absurd it is that Belgium should fondly conceive herself to be the center of International Jurispru-

15. That is, a balancing machine.
16. These treaties of Nijmegen (1679) and Ryswick (1697), both signed on Dutch soil, ended major wars in which Holland was part of the winning coalition.
17. Literally, "high politics"; Treitschke is referring here to the realm of power politics.

dence. As certainly as that public law is founded on practice, it follows that a State which occupies an abnormal position will form an abnormal conception of International Law. Belgium is neutral; it is by its nature an emasculated State. Is such a State likely to develop a healthy notion of International Law? I beg you to keep this consideration firmly in your minds hereafter, when you are confronted with the mass of Belgian literature on this subject. On the other hand, there exists to-day another State, which fancies itself in the position of being able to make an attack at any moment, and which is consequently the stronghold of barbarism in International Law. It is the fault of England alone that the provisions of International Law which relate to maritime warfare still sanction the practice of privileged piracy. So we are brought to realize that, since reciprocity is the very basis of International Law, it is of no use to hold up vague phrases and doctrines of humanity as the rule of conduct for States to follow; all theory must be founded on practice; only then does an understanding become genuinely reciprocal. That is a true balance of the Powers.

If we are to avoid misconception concerning the significance of International Law, we must bear in mind that all the International Law in the world cannot alter the essential nature of the State. No State can reasonably be called upon to agree to something which would amount to suicide. Even in the State-system, every individual State must still preserve its own sovereignty; even in its intercourse with other States, the preservation of this sovereignty is still its highest duty. The enduring provisions of International Law are those which do not affect sovereignty, that is to say, those concerned with ceremonial and with international private law. In time of peace it is hardly probable that these rights will be infringed; if they are, such infringements will be immediately expiated. Anyone who, even superficially, attacks the honor of a State, challenges by his action the very nature of the State. To reproach a State for having a too irritable sense of honor is to fail to appreciate the moral laws of politics. A State must have a very highly-developed sense of honor, if it is not to be disloyal to its own nature. The State is not a violet blooming in the shade. Its power must stand forth proud and refulgent, and it must not allow this power to be disputed, even in matters of forms and symbols. If the flag of the State is insulted, it is the duty of the State to demand satisfaction, and, if satisfaction is not forthcoming, to declare war, however trivial the occasion may appear; for the State must strain every nerve to preserve for itself that respect which it enjoys in the State-system.

From this it also follows that the limitations which States impose upon themselves by means of treaties are voluntary self-limitations, and that all treaties are concluded with the mental reservation *rebus sic stantibus*.[18] There never has been a State, and there never will be a State, which, in concluding a treaty, seriously intended to keep it forever. No State is in a position to conclude a treaty (which necessarily implies a certain limitation of its sovereignty) for all time to come. The State always has in mind the possibility of annulling the treaty at some future date; and indeed the treaty is only valid so long as the conditions under which it was made have not entirely altered. This idea has been declared inhuman, but actually it is humane. Only if the State knows that all its treaties have only a conditional validity, will it make its treaties wisely. History is not meant to be considered from the standpoint of a judge presiding over a civil lawsuit. From this point of view Prussia, since she had signed the Tilsit treaty,[19] ought not to have attacked Napoleon in 1813. But this treaty, too, was con-cluded *rebus sic stantibus*; and the circumstances (thank God!) had fundamentally changed even in those few years. A noble nation was given the opportunity of freeing itself from an insupportable slavery; and, as soon as a nation perceives such an opportunity, it is justified in daring to take advantage of it.

We must never lose sight in politics of the free moral forces of national life. No State in the world is to renounce that egotism which belongs to its sovereignty. If conditions are imposed on a State which would degrade it, to which it could not adhere, these conditions will be more honored in the breach than in the observance. History reveals one very beautiful fact: that a State recovers more easily from material losses than from attacks upon its honor. The loss of a province may be endured as a necessity imposed by prudence; but to endure under compulsion a state of slavery is an ever-open wound to a noble people. Napoleon, by the constant presence of his troops on Prussian soil, infused a glowing hatred into the veins of the most long-suffering. When a State is conscious that its honor has been insulted, the renunciation of a treaty is only a question of time. England and France experienced this in 1870, after the Crimean War, when they had arrogantly imposed upon exhausted Russia the condition that Russian warships should no longer be allowed in the Black Sea; and, when Russia took advantage of the good opportunity afforded by the Franco-German War to renounce this treaty, with the tacit support of Germany, she was doing no more than was morally justifiable.

When a State realizes that existing treaties no longer express the actual relations between the Powers, then, if it cannot bring the other contracting State to acquiescence by friendly negotiations, there is nothing for it but the international lawsuit War. Under such circumstances, a State declares war with the consciousness of fulfilling an absolute duty. No motives of personal gain are involved. The protagonists have simply perceived that existing treaties no longer correspond with their actual

18. "In these circumstances"; that is, Treitschke is claiming that there is no obligation to adhere to the terms of treaties when circumstances change.

19. There were actually two treaties of Tilsit signed within two days of one another in 1807. Treitschke is referring to the second, concluded June 9 between France and Prussia, in which the latter was forced to surrender nearly half its territory to neighboring French client states, as well as to pay a sizable indemnity to France.

relations, and, since the matter cannot be decided peaceably, it must be decided by the great international lawsuit War. The justice of war depends simply on the consciousness of a moral necessity. Since there cannot be, and ought not to be, any arbitrary power placed above the great personalities which we call nations, and since history must be in an eternal flux, war is justified. War must be conceived as an institution ordained of God. A State may, of course, form a mistaken judgment concerning the inevitability of war. Niebuhr says truly: "War does not establish any right that did not already exist." Individual acts of violence are expiated in the very moment that they are performed. It was thus that the unity of Germany and of Italy were achieved. On the other hand, not every war has an inevitable result, and the historian must therefore preserve an open mind; he must remember that the lives of States are counted in centuries. The proud saying of the vanquished Piedmontese, "We begin again"[20] will always have its place in the history of noble nations.

War will never be expelled from the world by international courts of arbitration. In any great question which concerns a nation's life it is simply impossible for the other members of the State-system to remain impartial. They must be partial, because they are members of a living community, mutually bound together or held apart by a diversity of interests. Supposing that such a foolish thing were possible as that Germany should allow the question of Alsace-Lorraine to be decided by a court of arbitration, which of the European nations would be capable of viewing the question impartially? Such a thing is not to be dreamed of. Hence the well-known fact that International Congresses are able to formulate the results of a war, and to decide upon it juridically, but that they are powerless to avert a war that is threatening. It is only in questions of the third rank that a foreign State can possibly be impartial.

Source: H.W.C. Davis, The Political Thought of Heinrich von Treitschke *(London: Constable and Company, 1914), 173–79.*

MAZZINI

EXCERPTS FROM GIUSEPPE MAZZINI, *AN ESSAY ON THE DUTIES OF MAN ADDRESSED TO WORKINGMEN* (1858)

Giuseppe Mazzini (1805–72) was born in Genoa and was involved in various liberal and nationalist organizations from a young age. In 1831 he formed a secret society called Young Italy, dedicated to Italian unification; within two years it had a membership of some 60,000, mainly from the cities of northern Italy. Again and again he spearheaded efforts to overthrow Austrian-backed regimes in Italy, and at one point was named part of a triumvirate governing a "Republic of Italy" created during the Revolutions of 1848. However, these all failed, and he spent much of the 1830s and 1840s in exile in Switzerland, Paris, and London. In 1844 he began writing his most famous work, An Essay on the Duties of Man Addressed to Workingmen, *in which he made the intellectual and spiritual case for liberal nationalism, based on the principles of republicanism and political and social equality. When Italy was finally united in 1861 under the rule of King Victor Emmanuel II of Piedmont, Mazzini wanted nothing to do with it, turning down a seat in the new Italian Chamber of Deputies and even attempting a rebellion in Sicily in 1870, for which he was briefly imprisoned. The king, however, granted an amnesty to his political opponents, and Mazzini settled in Pisa, where he died in 1872.*

Chapter V: Duties to Your Country

Your first duties—first as regards importance—are, as I have already told you, towards Humanity. You are men before you are either citizens or fathers. If

---

20. The Kingdom of Sardinia-Piedmont sought to create a unified Italy in 1848 by launching a war against Austria to drive the Habsburgs from the Italian provinces of Lombardy and Venetia. The result was failure, leading to the promise to "begin again." In 1859 the Piedmontese got another chance, and this time, with the support of France, they were able to defeat the Austrians, and then go on to create the Kingdom of Italy.

you do not embrace the whole human family in your affection; if you do not bear witness to your belief in the Unity of that family, consequent upon the Unity of God, and in that fraternity among the peoples which is destined to reduce that Unity to action; if, wheresoever a fellow-creature suffers, or the dignity of human nature is violated by false-hood or tyranny—you are not ready, if able, to aid the unhappy, and do not feel called upon to combat, if able, for the redemption of the betrayed and oppressed—you violate your law of life, you comprehend not that Religion which will be the guide and blessing of the future.

But what can each of you, singly, do for the moral improvement and progress of Humanity? You can from time to time give sterile utterance to your belief; you may, on some rare occasions, perform some act of charity towards a brother-man not belonging to your own land—no more. But charity is not the watchword of the Faith of the Future. The watchword of the faith of the future is Association and fraternal cooperation towards a common aim; and this is far superior to all charity, as the edifice which all of you should unite to raise would be superior to the humble hut each one of you might build alone, or with the mere assistance of lending and borrowing stone, mortar, and tools.

But, you tell me, you cannot attempt united action, distinct and divided as you are in language, customs, tendencies, and capacity. The individual is too insignificant, and Humanity too vast. The mariner of Brittany prays to God as he puts to sea; "Help me, my God! my boat is so small and Thy ocean so wide!" And this prayer is the true expression of the condition of each one of you, until you find the means of infinitely multiplying your forces and powers of action.

This means was provided for you by God when He gave you a country; when, even as a wise overseer of labour distributes the various branches of employment according to the different capaci-ties of the workmen, he divided Humanity into distinct groups or nuclei upon the face of the earth, thus creating the germ of nationalities. Evil

governments have disfigured the Divine design. Nevertheless you may still trace it, distinctly marked out—at least as far as Europe is con-cerned—by the course of the great rivers, the direction of the higher mountains, and other geographical conditions. They have disfigured it by their conquests, their greed, and their jealousy even of the righteous power of others; disfigured it so far that, if we except England and France, there is not perhaps a single country whose present boundaries correspond to that design.

These governments did not, and do not, recog-nize any country save their own families or dynasty, the egoism of caste. But the Divine design will infallibly be realized; natural divisions and the spontaneous, innate tendencies of the peoples will take the place of the arbitrary divisions, sanctioned by evil governments. The map of Europe will be redrawn. The countries of the peoples, defined by the vote of free men, will arise upon the ruins of the countries of kings and privileged castes, and between these countries harmony and fraternity will exist. And the common work of Humanity, of general amelioration, and the gradual discovery and application of its Law of life, being distributed according to local and general capacities, will be wrought out in peaceful and progressive develop-ment and advance. Then may each one of you, fortified by the power and affection of many millions, all speaking the same language, gifted with the same tendencies, and educated by the same historical tradition, hope even by your own single efforts to be able to benefit all Humanity.

O, my brothers, love your Country! Our country is our Home, a house God has given us, placing therein a numerous family that loves us, and whom we love; a family with whom we sympathize more readily and whom we understand more quickly than we do others; and which, from its being centered around a given spot, and from the homo-geneous nature of its elements, is adapted to a special branch of activity. Our Country is our common workshop, whence the products of our activity are sent forth for the benefit of the whole world; wherein the tools and implements of labor we can most usefully employ are gathered together; nor may we reject them without disobeying the plan of the Almighty, and diminishing our own strength.

In laboring for our own country on the right principle, we labor for Humanity. Our country is the fulcrum of the lever we have to wield for the common good. If we abandon the fulcrum, we run the risk of rendering ourselves useless not only to Humanity but to our country itself. Before men can associate with the nations of which Humanity is composed, they must have a national existence. There is no true association except among equals. It is only through our country that we can have a recognized collective existence. Humanity is a vast army advancing to the conquest of lands unknown, against enemies both powerful and astute. The peoples are the different corps, the divisions of that army. Each of them has its post assigned to it, and its special operation to execute; and the common victory depends upon the exactitude with which those distinct operations are fulfilled. Disturb not the order of battle. Forsake not the banner given to you by God. Wheresoever you may be, in the center of whatsoever people circumstances may have placed you, be ever ready to combat for the liberty of that people, should it be necessary, but combat in such wise that the blood you shed may reflect glory, not on yourself alone, but on your country. Say not I, but We. Let each man among you strive to incarnate his country in himself. Let each man among you regard himself as a guarantor, responsible for his fellow-countrymen, and learn so to govern his actions as to cause his country to be loved and respected through him. Your country is the sign of the Mission God has given you to fulfill towards Humanity. The faculties and forces of all her sons should be associated in the accomplishment of that mission. The true country is a community of free men and equals, bound together in fraternal concord to labor towards a common aim. You are bound to make it and to maintain it such. The country is not an aggregation, but an association. There is, therefore, no true country without a uniform right. There is no true country where the uniformity of that right is violated by the existence of caste privilege and inequality. Where the activity of a portion of the powers and faculties of the individual is either cancelled or dormant; where there is not a common Principle, recognized, accepted, and developed by all, there is no true Nation, no People; but only a multitude, a fortuitous agglomeration of men whom circumstances have called together and whom circumstances may again divide. In the name of the love you bear your country, you must peacefully but untiringly combat the existence of privilege and inequality in the land that gave you life.

There is but one sole legitimate privilege, the privilege of Genius when it reveals itself united with virtue. But this is a privilege given by God, and when you acknowledge it, and follow its inspiration, you do so freely, exercising your own reason and your own choice. Every privilege which demands submission from you in virtue of power, inheritance, or any other right than the Right common to all, is a usurpation and a tyranny which you are bound to resist and destroy.

Be your country your Temple: God at the summit; a people of equals at the base.

Accept no other formula, no other moral law, if you would not dishonor alike your country and yourselves. Let all secondary laws be but the gradual regulation of your existence by the progressive application of this Supreme law. And in order that they may be such, it is necessary that all of you should aid in framing them. Laws framed only by a single fraction of the citizens, can never, in the very nature of things, be other than the mere expression of the thoughts, aspirations, and desires of that fraction; the representation, not of the country, but of a third or fourth part, of a class or zone of the country.

The laws should be the expression of the universal aspiration, and promote the universal good. They should be a pulsation of the heart of the nation. The entire nation should, either directly or indirectly, legislate.

The entire nation
should legislate!

By yielding up this mission into the hands of a few, you substitute the selfishness of one class for the Country, which is the union of all classes.

Country is not only a mere zone of territory. The true Country is the Idea to which it gives birth; it is the Thought of love, the sense of communion which unites in one all the sons of that territory.

So long as a single one amongst your brothers has no vote to represent him in the development of the national life, so long as there is one left to vegetate in ignorance where others are educated, so long as a single man, able and willing to work, languishes in poverty through want of work to do, you have no country in the sense in which Country ought to exist—the country of all and for all.

Education, labor, and the franchise, are the three main pillars of the Nation; rest not until you have built them thoroughly up with your own labor and exertions.

Be it yours to evolve the life of your country in loveliness and strength; free from all servile fears or skeptical doubts; maintaining as its basis the People; as its guide the principles of its Religious Faith, logically and energetically applied; its strength, the united strength of all; its aim, the fulfillment of the mission given to it by God.

And so long as you are ready to die for Humanity, the life of your country will be immortal.

Source: Hanover Historical Texts Project, http:// history.hanover.edu/texts/mazzini/mazzini5.html, accessed July 1, 2014.

DANILEVSKII
EXCERPTS FROM NIKOLAI IAKOVLEVICH DANILEVSKII, *RUSSIA AND EUROPE* (1879)

Nikolai Iakovlevich Danilevskii (1822–85) was a Russian naturalist, economist, ethnologist, philosopher, and historian. He was the most important theorist of pan-Slavism—that is, the idea that all the world's Slavs should be united under Russian leadership. His ideas were deeply influential among the educated Russian middle class.

From Chapter 13: The Place of Austria

Both Turkey and Austria have lost all meaning. Never having an internal basis or reason to exist, they have now lost the temporary and accidental significance justifying their political existence. In other words they have died, and like any carcass, they are dangerously unhygienic, producing their own kind of illness and contagion. Almost everyone agrees that Turkey has died, but a clear view of things shows that Austria is just as dead, and neither centralization nor dualism, neither simply Austrian nor Austrian-Turkish federalism will revive it. With the disappearance of the historical idea that grouped these people-elements into a political body, these elements will become free and can only be brought together again by the action of a new living principle which, according to the predominant, supreme significance of nationality in any type of political combinations (from the integral, condensed state to the entire political system) can be none other than the ethnographic principle. In the present case, this principle can only be the idea of Slavdom: not any particular idea of an Austrian, Turkish, or Austro-Turkish kind of Slavdom, but the idea of *All-Slavdom*. . . .

. . . By ethnographic conditions, the Slavs must form a federation, but this federation must encompass all lands and peoples from the Adriatic Sea to the Pacific Ocean, from the Arctic Sea to the Archipelago [i.e., the Aegean Sea]. In compliance with these conditions, and also in accordance with the facts of history and with the political situation right next to the powerful, hostile Germanic-Roman world, this federation would have to be as closely-knit as possible, under the leadership and hegemony of a whole, united Russian state. Such an All-Slavic federation fully meeting the requirements of the ethnographic principle, like any complete answer to the question, simultaneously abolishes all other incompatibilities and hindrances that arise in our minds at every turn for the Austrian or Austro-Turkish federations.

And into this All-Slavic federation must enter, willingly or unwillingly, all those non-Slavic nationalities (Greeks, Romanians, and Magyars) crammed into the Slavic body, whose historical fate has been inseparably connected, for better or for worse, with ours. But this foreign ethnographic admixture losing itself, so to speak, in the mass of the Slavs, cannot have the same harmful, disintegrative influence for an All-Slavic union that it has had for individual Slavic unions. Not only that, but the main non-Slavic members of the Slavic federation—the Greeks and Romanians—cannot even be considered a foreign admixture within it, because whatever they lack in similarity of the blood is made up for by their similarity of spirit: though not Slavs, they are Orthodox. But even that is not all. These peoples are not so foreign to Slavs, even by blood, as some think and as many would like. They are saturated, so to speak, with Slavic elements, and as a link in the system of Slavic peoples are analogous to the Romanic peoples within the European system who, like the French, are saturated with Germanic elements. What is strictly non-Slavic in them is only the vain pretense of isolation, exaggerated within their intelligentsia by the temptations, instigations, and incitements of our Western ill-wishers. . . . Concerning the Magyars, the saying applies: "Take the smooth with the rough." Having encroached on Slavic lands, and having acquired the completely unjustified sovereignty over them that they have enjoyed over the course of several centuries, they must share the fate of all great tribes and exchange primacy and a ruling position for secondary, subject status. . . .

And so, an All-Slavic federation is the only reasonable, and thus the only resolution of the Eastern Question.[21] But before we can examine it in detail and answer all objections that could be made against it, and have been made by both friends and enemies, we must turn all our attention to one of the most essential elements of this question which we have not yet touched upon, but which can be justly considered its Gordian knot. It would be preferable not to cut this knot, but untie it: that is, to resolve it correctly (or in other words, in compliance with the inherent, essential requirements of the matter). I have in mind the question of Constantinople.

From Chapter 14: Tsargrad [Constantinople]

. . . Neither the great Western powers, nor Greece, would derive any benefit from the possession of Constantinople, and not only that, but it would even be such a heavy burden that it would be hard for the first to bear, and would inevitably crush the second.

For Russia the possession of Constantinople appears in a completely different light. The advantages it would gain from it are truly priceless and innumerable.

1) Recent bitter experience[22] has shown where is [vulnerability to the south] the Achilles' heel of Russia, which its enemies have long sought. In contrast, the most decisive experience of many centuries, undertaken with huge means and under the leadership of the most skillful operators, had shown very clearly that from the other sides, the west and the north, it is invulnerable. The vulnerability from the east has already passed; thus all that remains is vulnerability to the south. These are not just empirical data, but facts supporting the most satisfactory explanation, since they result from the situation of Russia, the essential characteristics and particular nature of its power and strength.

Any attack from the west would be repulsed by the land forces of Russia, which always have, and always will constitute the main source of its power. Vast, impassable swamps and forests divide the expanse along the western border of Russia into

---

21. The Eastern Question first emerged in the late eighteenth century, and concerned the fate of lands in the Middle East and southeastern Europe as the Ottoman Empire lost its hold over those territories.

22. Namely, the Crimean War of 1854–56, when the Ottomans granted free access through the straits to their British and French allies, allowing them to invade Russian territory.

two completely separate theaters of military action. A simultaneous attack on them both is possible only in the highly unlikely event of an alliance between both our western neighbors, Prussia and Austria. Thus, in most cases Russia can be completely at peace either in the region to the south, or to the north of the woodlands and swamp system of the Pripiat River. Our weak point on that side, of course, is Poland; but our political relations with it are such that in any war with Poland, the mightiest of our neighbors, Prussia, could never be among our enemies, at least not for long. But Russia's strength consists not only in its army but in the soul of its whole people, which has always been ready to see its homes and property in the embrace of flames rather than enemy hands. And any enemy invading Russian territory would have to contend with this people.

From the Baltic Sea can only come diversions, incidental attacks at one or another point; but it cannot serve as the basis for a proper, systematically organized action, for the simple reason that any success made in summer must be left off in wintertime.

South From the south, on the contrary, Russia is open to the attacks of powers with great naval means. A land defense of the coasts requires vast forces, though actually even that is not enough. To have any kind of success, enemies would have to hold it and turn it into a new point of support for further ventures. Of course, an invasion into the interior of Russia even from this side would be difficult, even impossible if you will but there would be no need for such an invasion. Possession of the sea coasts,—or even of the Crimea alone, would be enough to bring real harm to Russia and paralyze it. The possession of Constantinople and the straits would eliminate this danger and make the southern border of Russia the most safe and impregnable.

2) We have fallen into the unfortunate habit of saying that Russia is big enough, or even too big; that it needs no more conquests; that new acquisitions would be a burden to it, and already are a burden to it. Of course there are different kinds of acquisitions, but concerning general complaints about the too-vast expanse of Russia I see no grounds for complaint. England after all is bigger than Russia,[23] and it is not burdened by its far-flung possessions scattered all over the face of the earth. And concepts of size and greatness are all relative, and it seems to me a correct determination can only be made by the relationship between the size attained and the expansive force within what is growing. A big fat oak fifteen *sazhens*[24] high must not be called too big when it has only assumed its normal dimensions. Likewise a state cannot be considered to have reached full size, no matter how many square miles or *versts*[25] it is, when nearly four million of the ruling people's fellow tribesmen live outside of it. It has only reached full size when the entire people that formed it, supports it, and brings it life has united together, and when it has become the undisputed lord of the lands settled by this people; that is, it controls the access into and out of it, the mouths of the rivers that water almost its full extent, and the mouths of its inland seas. Put simply, when it has accomplished its historical purpose. Speaking of the expanse of Russia, we should not forget that, soil-wise and climate-wise, it is situated in less than ideal conditions than all the great states of Europe, Asia, and America, and thus it requires a greater expanse than they do to gather the makings of its wealth and might.

Of course the great expanse has its own disadvantages, and without a doubt the main one is the great extent of its borders. But the acquisition of Constantinople would give Russia a completely different advantage which, instead of increasing its disadvantages, would decrease them to a significant degree, condensing, so to speak, twenty-five

23. Danilevskii is including in "England" all of the British Empire, which at the time of his writing encompassed over 425,000 square miles—50,000 more square miles than the entirety of the Russian Empire.

24. About thirty-five meters.

25. A *verst* is 500 *sazhens*, or just over a kilometer.

hundred [*versts*] of borderlines all along the Black and Azov Seas into a single point. Therefore, if Constantinople in the hands of England or France would require a sizable army and navy to defend this point, over and above what they would need without it, in the hands of Russia it would allow a reduction of its armed forces and attending expenditures by at least the same amount. . . .

So from whatever side we approach the matter, an All-Slavic federation with Russia at the head and its capital at Tsargrad is the only reasonable, intelligent solution to the great historical puzzle passed down from ancient times, known as the Eastern Question. . . .

Being face to face with a West that is hostile to them is the reason that would make the Slavs wish for very close federative bonds beneath the political hegemony and leadership of Russia, which has the most legal right to it, based on its comparative strength over all the other members of the Slavic family, and based on its having maintained political independence over the course of many centuries. Despite the places where Russia swerved from the path of healthy politics, especially in the last half of the era of Catherine, still it and only it among all the Slavic states could not only preserve its independence under the most unfavorable circumstances but even unite nearly all of the Russian people and form the mightiest state in the world.

But for the political strength of the All-Slavic union, it is not enough to grant Russia undisputed hegemonic dominion over it; the secondary groups or members of the union must also provide sufficient guarantee of the power and unity of its inner structure. The divisiveness to which the Austrian Slavs are particularly inclined, from having long lived under the ruling principle of *Divide et impera*,[26] must spill over the borders of the largest

"Russia is the best" [handwritten marginal note]

linguistic and ethnographic groups into which they are divided. Dividing by minor tribal identities, each easily tempted by pretensions to political independence, would have the essential problem that each of these minor entities would have too little incentive to devote all their strength to the burdens that come with such a great political role. . . .

Thus, corresponding to the main ethnographic groups into which the Slavic world divides, as well as the tribes included by place of residence, but also mostly according to actual, genuine moral inclinations—the All-Slavic union must consist of the following states:

The Russian Empire with Galicia and Ugric Rus[27] annexed to it.

A Czecho-Moravian-Slovakian kingdom consisting, besides Czechia,[28] of Moravia and the northwest part of Hungary settled exclusively or predominantly by Slovaks; approximately nine million in population and 1,800 square miles of territory.

A Serbo-Croat-Slovene kingdom consisting of the Serbian Principality, Montenegro, Bosnia, Herzegovina, Old Serbia, northern Albania, the Voivodeship of Serbia and Banat of Temeschwar, Croatia, Slavonia, Dalmatia, the Military Frontier [of Austria], the Duchy of Carniola, Goritzia and Gradisca, Istria, the Trieste region, two-thirds of Carinthia, and one-fifth of Styria on the Drava; approximately eight million in population and 4,500 square miles of territory.

A Bulgarian kingdom with Bulgaria and most of Rumelia and Macedonia; approximately 6–7 million in population and more than 3,000 square miles.

A Romanian kingdom with Wallachia, Moldavia, part of Bukovina, approximately half of Transylvania along the Maros River, the western borders of Bessarabia populated predominantly by Moldavians, in exchange for which Russia must

26. Latin for "divide and conquer"; that is, Danilevskii is claiming that the Habsburgs have intentionally set against one another the various Slavic groups under their rule, so as better to keep them under control.

27. Ruthenia, at that time part of Hungary.
28. That is, Bohemia.

receive from it part of southern Bessarabia from the Danube delta and Dobruja. This would consist of nearly seven million in population and more than 3,000 square miles.

A Hellenic kingdom including present-day Thessaly, Epirus, the southwestern part of Macedonia, all the islands of the Archipelago [Aegean Islands], Rhodes, Crete, Cyprus, and the Aegean coast of Asia Minor; with over four million in population and 2,800 to 3,000 square miles.

A Magyar kingdom, that is, Hungary and Transylvania beyond those parts not settled by Magyar tribes, which must go to Russia, Czechia, Serbia, and Romania; approximately seven million in population and 3,000 square miles.

The Tsargrad district with the parts of Romania and Asia Minor surrounding the Bosporus, the Sea of Marmara and the Dardanelles, with the peninsula of Gallipoli and the island of Tenedos; with a population of approximately two million.

A union like this—of peoples mostly related by spirit and blood, a fresh one hundred twenty-five million in population, with Tsargrad at the natural center of its moral and material unity—would give the only full, reasonable, and thus the only possible, solution to the Eastern Question. Owning only what belongs to it by right, not threatening anyone and not fearing any threat, it could withstand all storms and adversity while calmly proceeding down the path of independent development, in the fullness of its peoples' strength, and in the most harmonious coordination of the kindred elements comprising it. Corresponding to its ethnographic makeup, religious illumination, and historical background, it would form a unique cultural-historical type, strengthened by a long struggle against the hostile outside forces now separating its peoples, a struggle without which it cannot be formed. . . .

From Chapter 15: The All-Slavic Union

. . . Not belonging in essence to Europe, Russia by its own standards is an anomaly in the Germanic-Roman world of Europe, and the natural increase in the size of its population must reinforce its position as an anomaly. By its very existence Russia throws off the whole system of European equilibrium. Not one state would dare to make war against Russia one-on-one. The Eastern War[29] showed this best of all, when four states, with the help of Austria (more than half of which took a hostile attitude toward Russia), with the most disadvantageous conditions for us and the most advantageous for them, still took a whole year to besiege a single coastal fortress [i.e., Sevastopol, in the Crimean War], without any kind of Frederick, Suvorov,[30] or Napoleon on the Russian side, but only the immense capabilities of Russia and the unconquerable spirit of its defenders.

We must not fail to realize that Russia is too big and powerful to be only one of the great European powers, and if it could play that role for these last seventy years, it was only by contorting or crimping its own natural aspirations, not giving them free rein, and deviating from its own destiny. This self-denigration must grow progressively in proportion to its natural development of strength, since by the very essence of the matter, the expansive force of Russia is much greater than that of the states of Europe, and its disproportion with the demands of the policy of equilibrium will necessarily become more and more painfully obvious. In saying so, I am of course looking at the matter from a general point of view, but not in application to any particular case, when due to the confluence of various circumstances a weaker opponent can rule over one much stronger. Any investigations of this sort certainly presuppose the caveat expressed in the oft-used formula, "All other conditions being equal."

However, considering the proximity of Europe, considering the boundary line shared with Europe across thousands of *versts*, the complete separation of Russia from Europe is inconceivable. That kind of separation could not protect China and

29. That is, the Crimean War.
30. Alexander Suvorov (1730–1800) was a successful Russian general of the late eighteenth century.

Japan,[31] separated from Europe by the earth's diameter. Russia must have some kind of direct relations with it. If it cannot and must not be in an intimate, kindred connection with Europe as a member of the European family (which the evidence of long experience proves will not accept it, but will only demand an impossible rejection of its most obvious rights, healthy interests, natural sympathies, and holy obligations); and if, on the other hand, it does not want to be in a position of submission to Europe (reconfiguring its desires accordingly and fulfilling all Europe's humiliating demands), then there is nothing left for it to do but assume its actual role, designated by ethnographic and historical conditions, and serve as a counterweight not to one or another European state, but to Europe in general, in its totality.

But however great and powerful Russia is, it is still too weak to do this. It needs to weaken the enemy, separate those who are its enemies against their will, and turn them to its side as friends. Russia's lot is a happy one: To increase its power, it does not need to conquer or oppress, like all the other powers on earth up to now (Macedonia, Rome, the Arabs, the Mongols, and states of the Germanic-Roman world), but to liberate and restore. And in this marvelous near-coincidence of moral conviction and obligation with political advantage and necessity, we must not fail to see the guarantee of the fulfillment of its great destiny, assuming our world is not a pitiful, accidental mess but a reflection of the highest reason, truth, and kindness.

We should not deceive ourselves. Europe's hostility is too obvious: it lies not in the accidental combinations of European policies, not in the ambitions of one or another statesman, but in its most fundamental interests. Its internal accounts are far from settled. The seeds of internal struggle have begun to germinate in recent times, but these

are most likely among the last. Once they are settled, or pacified for an extended length of time, Europe will again direct all its forces and designs against Russia, which it considers its natural-born enemy. If Russia does not understand its significance, it will inevitably suffer the fate of everything outdated, superfluous, and unnecessary. With its historical role gradually diminishing, Russia will have to bow its head to the demands of Europe, which will not grant it any influence in the East, and will erect (in one form or another, depending on circumstances) strongholds against its connections with its western Slavic relatives. Not only this, but, on the one hand, with the help of its accomplices among the Turks, Germans, Magyars, Italians, Poles, Greeks, and maybe even Romanians (who are always ready to break away from disunited Slavdom), and on the other hand, by its political and civilizational temptations, Europe will so remove the very soul of Slavdom that it breaks out in the bloom of Europeanism, with Europe itself fertilizing the soil. But for Russia—having not fulfilled its calling and thus having lost the reason for its existence, its vital essence, its idea—there will be nothing left but ingloriously to live out its pitiful life, to rot through like historical rubbish lacking all sense and significance, or to turn into a lifeless mass, an inanimate body, so to speak; and also, in the best case, to dissolve into ethnographic material for new, unknown historical formations, leaving no living trace of itself.

Being foreign to the European world by its inherent constitution, and besides that, being too strong and powerful to be merely one member of the European family or just another of the great European powers, Russia can only take a place in history worthy of itself and Slavdom by being the head of its own independent political system of states, and serving as a counterbalance to Europe in general and as a whole. This is the advantage, the benefit, and the whole idea of the All-Slavic union in regard to Russia. . . .

The other bogeyman that scares people away from the idea of All-Slavdom is the danger of global

---

31. In the nineteenth century, China and Japan were both subject to aggression from Europeans and Americans seeking trade.

monarchy, the fear of world domination. As was made clear in the explanation just given, even if such world domination were a natural and necessary consequence of the All-Slavic union, then in any case it would be not especially Russian, but All-Slavic, domination—and to the Slavs, it would seem, there is nothing to fear. The ancient Romans were not afraid of the idea of global domination; England has no fear of the idea of global domination of the seas, and the expansion of its possessions, girdling the seas and oceans with a chain of large and small British colonies; even America is not afraid of the idea of unchallenged dominion from Greenland to Tierra del Fuego. What strange kind of modesty is this: to back away from a great future and avoid it for fear of becoming too powerful and strong . . . ?

But that is not the point. This fear itself has no basis at all. A great Slavic union guaranteeing the freedom of the Slavs and their fruitful interaction with each other could not threaten anyone's independence or anyone's legal rights. Once again, a simple statistical calculation will confirm this. The population of only those parts of Europe that at the present time play an active political role—that is, Germany (after the apportionment of all the non-German parts of Austria), France, and England, with the addition of Belgium and Holland, which willingly or not always end up following them—would equal the population of the whole Slavic union. Including Italy, Spain, Portugal, and the Scandinavian states would create an excess on the European side of at least fifty million people. Thus from the outset the Slavic system of states would still be significantly weaker than the European system of states by the amount of its population, and could only be considered insuperable in terms of the defense and protection of Slavic independence and autonomy. The balance of power would be equalized somewhat by the above-cited strategic locations of Constantinople and the Czech bastion.

But considering the abundant love of humanity in the Slavic heart, which considers it a most sacred obligation to sacrifice its own Slavic goals and interests to some unknown set of all-human goals (which, due to the most absurd habit of confusing this "all-human" with "Western" and "European," goes only to the benefit of the European, which is always hostile to the Slavic), we must not limit ourselves to the preceding evidence. We need to show that not only the independence, but the political power of the Slavs is vitally necessary for the lawful and harmonious course of intra-human interactions; that the political power of Slavdom not only cannot threaten the enslavement of the whole world or world domination, but only this can put up an adequate barrier against the world domination that more and more is being acquired (and to a significant degree, already has been) by Europe. . . .

. . . With the unification of all the major European nationalities, and thus the near-complete elimination of the pretexts and temptations to destroy the political system of equilibrium, all the former hindrances to the spread of European dominion over other parts of the world have now fallen.

Having been a force from the very beginning of European history; strengthened by its religious fanaticism and militancy, Islam collapsed, along with the spirit of its followers. The immensity, massiveness, and/or remoteness of such political bodies as China and Japan in eastern Asia lost their defensive significance once steam power was applied to military purposes, since now it became possible to transport to the opposite hemisphere a mass of troops strong enough for a rapid and energetic suppression of any uprising that might occur, and even to take these troops deep within the country by means of rivers. Finally the truest obstacle to Europe's world domination—the internal struggles of European states to establish proper relations among themselves—has also been eliminated by the near-complete attainment of stable equilibrium. All the ambitious activity of Europe (of which there has been no lack) is to an increasing degree directed toward what is not

Europe, as was always the case during a truce in its internal struggle. The *Drang nach Osten*[32] is not long in turning from word into deed.

Fortunately, just as the old obstacles to Europe's world domination had fallen, there arose two new ones, and only they had the ability to stop it in its path, and lay the foundation of true global equilibrium. These two obstacles are the United States of America and Russia. But the first is insulated from the interference of Europe by the barriers of the New World, and because of its position is comparatively less interested in how to handle the Old World, and also cannot in and of itself have a great influence on this theater of activity. Thus the full burden of preserving the balance of powers in the Old World rests on the shoulders of Russia. But if the American states are strong enough to fulfill the task laid upon them, due to their overseas location, the same cannot be said of Russia.

The irreconcilable hostility of Europe toward Russia is proven by long experience, and from that we have every reason to believe that as soon as Europe puts the last of its affairs in order, when the new elements of its system's political equilibrium have time to settle down and get firmly established, then just as it was in the Eastern War, the first excuse will be enough for an attack on Russia. And excuses of this kind are always readily provided by the East and Poland.

But only a united Slavdom can contend with a united Europe. And so, an All-Slavic union does not threaten world domination, but on the contrary offers the necessary and at the same time only possible guarantee of preserving global equilibrium, as the only bulwark against the world domination of Europe. This union would be no threat to anyone, but a purely defensive measure not only in the particular interests of Slavdom, but for the whole world. The result of an All-Slavic

union would not be world domination, but an equal and proper division of power and influence among the peoples or groups of peoples that should be considered the active agents in the present era of world history—Europe, Slavdom, and America—which are each at different stages of development. . . .

From Chapter 16: The Struggle

Sooner or later, like it or not, a struggle with Europe (or at least a significant part of it) is inevitable, over the Eastern Question: that is, over the freedom and independence of Slavdom, over the possession of Tsargrad—over everything that Europe considers a matter of Russia's unruly ambition, but which every Russian worthy of the name considers a necessary requirement of its historical calling. The dreadful outbreak of the struggle may be delayed, postponed for one or another reason by us or by the Europeans, but it can only be prevented by Europe feeling the full justice of Slavic demands and voluntarily ceding them (of which there is little hope, as all can see); or by Russia actually showing itself to be, as its enemies say, "an ailing, failing colossus," weakened morally, ceasing to heed not only the voice of national honor but also the loudest summons of the instinct for self-preservation; ready to renounce all traditions of its history and disavow the very idea of its existence. But that is not all. Even if Russia went to such a level of self-abasement, it would be too unbelievable: they would see this as deception and a ruse, and would still not leave us in peace.

We consider the very process of this inevitable struggle, and not just certain of its desired outcomes (as we have repeatedly explained), salutary and beneficial, since only this struggle can sober our thoughts and raise in all levels of society the national spirit, which is sinking into imitativeness and worship of the foreign, infected by the extremely dangerous illness we call Europeanism. Perhaps we will be accused of preaching enmity or extolling war. Such an accusation would be incorrect. We are not preaching war, if for no other

---

32. German for "drive toward the East," an expression favored by German nationalists who sought to conquer and colonize eastern Europe.

reason than the fact that such a message would be only too funny from a voice as weak as ours. Yet we are affirming, and even proving, that a struggle is inevitable, and suggesting that even though war is a very great evil, there is still a greater one, something much worse than war, against which war can serve as medicine, since "man does not live by bread alone."[33] [. . .]

Source: Nikolai Iakovlevich Danilevskii, Russia and Europe: The Slavic World's Political and Cultural Relations with the Germanic-Roman West: The Slavic World's Political and Cultural Relations with the Germanic-Roman West, translated by Stephen M. Woodburn *(Bloomington, IN: Slavica, 2013)*, 313–15, 324–26, 332–33, 335–36, 344–46, 354–55, 364–65, 373–74.

ANGELL

EXCERPTS FROM NORMAN ANGELL, *THE GREAT ILLUSION* (1910)

English journalist Norman Angell was Paris editor for the London Daily Mail *from 1905 to 1912. In his most famous work,* The Great Illusion, *he argued that the economies of the European powers had become so closely intertwined that any war among them would be futile (although, contrary to some commenters, he never claimed that war had become impossible). He laid out his case in his introductory synopsis, which he wrote in the third person.*

What are the fundamental motives that explain the present rivalry of armaments in Europe, notably the Anglo-German? Each nation pleads the need for defence; but this implies that someone is likely to attack, and has therefore a presumed interest in so doing. What are the motives which each State thus fears its neighbors may obey?

They are based on the universal assumption that a nation, in order to find outlets for expanding population and increasing industry, or simply to ensure the best conditions possible for its people,

is necessarily pushed to territorial expansion and the exercise of political force against others (German naval competition is assumed to be the expression of the growing need of an expanding population for a larger place in the world, a need which will find a realization in the conquest of English Colonies or trade, unless these are defended); it is assumed, therefore, that a nation's relative prosperity is broadly determined by its political power; that nations being competing units, advantage, in the last resort, goes to the possessor of preponderant military force, the weaker going to the wall, as in the other forms of the struggle for life.

The author challenges this whole doctrine. He attempts to show that it belongs to a stage of development out of which we have passed; that the commerce and industry of a people no longer depend upon the expansion of its political frontiers; that a nation's political and economic frontiers do not now necessarily coincide; that military power is socially and economically futile, and can have no relation to the prosperity of the people exercising it; that it is impossible for one nation to seize by force the wealth or trade of another—to enrich itself by subjugating, or imposing its will by force on another; that, in short, war, even when victorious, can no longer achieve those aims for which peoples strive.

He establishes this apparent paradox, in so far as the economic problem is concerned, by showing that wealth in the economically civilized world is founded upon credit and commercial contract (these being the outgrowth of an economic interdependence due to the increasing division of labor and greatly developed communication). If credit and commercial contract are tampered with in an attempt at confiscation, the credit-dependent wealth is undermined, and its collapse involves that of the conqueror; so that if conquest is not to be self-injurious it must respect the enemy's property, in which case it becomes economically futile. Thus the wealth of conquered territory remains in the hands of the population of such

33. Matthew 4:4.

territory. When Germany annexed Alsatia *[Alsace-Lorraine]*, no individual German secured a single mark's worth of Alsatian property as the spoils of war. Conquest in the modern world is a process of multiplying by *x*, and then obtaining the original figure by dividing by *x*. For a modern nation to add to its territory no more adds to the wealth of the people of such nation than it would add to the wealth of Londoners if the City of London were to annex the county of Hertford.

The author also shows that international finance has become so interdependent and so interwoven with trade and industry that the intangibility of an enemy's property extends to his trade. It results that political and military power can in reality do nothing for trade; the individual merchants and manufacturers of small nations, exercising no such power, compete successfully with those of the great. Swiss and Belgian merchants drive English from the British Colonial market; Norway has, relatively to population, a greater mercantile marine than Great Britain; the public credit (as a rough-and-ready indication, among others, of security and wealth) of small States possessing no political power often stands higher than that of the Great Powers of Europe. . . .

The forces which have brought about the economic futility of military power have also rendered it futile as a means of enforcing a nation's moral ideals or imposing social institutions upon a conquered people. Germany could not turn Canada or Australia into German colonies—i.e., stamp out their language, law, literature, traditions, etc.—by "capturing" them. The necessary security in their material possessions enjoyed by the inhabitants of such conquered provinces, quick inter-communication by a cheap press, widely-read literature, enable even small communities to become articulate and effectively to defend their special social or moral possessions, even when military conquest has been complete. The fight for ideals can no longer take the form of fight between nations, because the lines of division on moral questions are within the nations themselves and intersect the political frontiers. There is no modern State which is completely Catholic or Protestant, or liberal or autocratic, or aristocratic or democratic, or socialist or individualist; the moral and spiritual struggles of the modern world go on between citizens of the same State in unconscious intellectual co-operation with corresponding groups in other States, not between the public powers of rival States.

This classification by strata involves necessarily a redirection of human pugnacity, based rather on the rivalry of classes and interests than on State divisions. War has no longer the justification that it makes for the survival of the fittest; it involves the survival of the less fit. The idea that the struggle between nations is a part of the evolutionary law of man's advance involves a profound misreading of the biological analogy.

The warlike nations do not inherit the earth; they represent the decaying human element. The diminishing rôle of physical force in all spheres of human activity carries with it profound psychological modifications.

These tendencies, mainly the outcome of purely modern conditions (e.g. rapidity of communication), have rendered the problems of modern international politics profoundly and essentially different from the ancient; yet our ideas are still dominated by the principles and axioms, images and terminology of the bygone days.

The author urges that these little-recognized facts may be utilized for the solution of the armament difficulty on at present untried lines—by such modification of opinion in Europe that much of the present motive to aggression will cease to be operative, and by thus diminishing the risk of attack, diminishing to the same extent the need for defence. He shows how such a political reformation is within the scope of practical politics, and the methods which should be employed to bring it about.

Source: Norman Angell, The Great Illusion *(London and New York: Putnam's Sons, 1910), 9–13.*

VON BERNHARDI
counter and rebuilt this argument

INTRODUCTION TO FRIEDRICH VON BERNHARDI, *GERMANY AND THE NEXT WAR* (1912)

Friedrich von Bernhardi was born in St. Petersburg, Russia, in 1849, but in 1851 he moved with his family to the German province of Silesia. He served with distinction in the Franco-Prussian War, and in the victory parade through Paris that followed he was given the honor of being the first German soldier to ride through the Arc de Triomphe. He held a variety of posts in the years that followed, including head of the military history department of the General Staff. In 1909, however, he retired from active service in order to focus on writing. In this, his most famous work, he made the controversial claim that war, far from being something to be avoided, was "a biological necessity."

Note that in this introduction Bernhardi focuses on the question of war in general. In the excerpts included in the "Supplemental Documents" section, he offers specific recommendations for German foreign and military policy.

Since 1795, when Immanuel Kant published in his old age his treatise on "Perpetual Peace," many have considered it an established fact that war is the destruction of all good and the origin of all evil. In spite of all that history teaches, no conviction is felt that the struggle between nations is inevitable, and the growth of civilization is credited with a power to which war must yield. But, undisturbed by such human theories and the change of times, war has again and again marched from country to country with the clash of arms, and has proved its destructive as well as creative and purifying power. It has not succeeded in teaching mankind what its real nature is. Long periods of war, far from convincing men of the necessity of war, have, on the contrary, always revived the wish to exclude war, where possible, from the political intercourse of nations.

This wish and this hope are widely disseminated even to-day. The maintenance of peace is lauded as the only goal at which statesmanship should aim. This unqualified desire for peace has obtained in our days a quite peculiar power over men's spirits. This aspiration finds its public expression in peace leagues and peace congresses; the Press of every country and of every party opens its columns to it. The current in this direction is, indeed, so strong that the majority of Governments profess— outwardly, at any rate—that the necessity of maintaining peace is the real aim of their policy; while when a war breaks out the aggressor is universally stigmatized, and all Governments exert themselves, partly in reality, partly in pretence, to extinguish the conflagration. . . .

This aspiration is directly antagonistic to the great universal laws which rule all life. War is a biological necessity of the first importance, a regulative element in the life of mankind which cannot be dispensed with, since without it an unhealthy development will follow, which excludes every advancement of the race, and therefore all real civilization. "War is the father of all things."[34] The sages of antiquity long before Darwin recognized this.

The struggle for existence is, in the life of Nature, the basis of all healthy development. All existing things show themselves to be the result of contesting forces. So in the life of man the struggle is not merely the destructive, but the life-giving principle. "To supplant or to be supplanted is the essence of life," says Goethe, and the strong life gains the upper hand. The law of the stronger holds good everywhere. Those forms survive which are able to procure themselves the most favourable conditions of life, and to assert themselves in the universal economy of Nature. The weaker succumb. This struggle is regulated and restrained by the unconscious sway of biological laws and by the interplay of opposite forces. In the plant world and the animal world this process is worked out in unconscious tragedy. In the human race it is consciously carried out, and regulated by social ordinances. The man of strong will and strong intellect tries by every means to assert himself, the ambitious strive

34. Heraclitus of Ephesus.

to rise, and in this effort the individual is far from being guided merely by the consciousness of right. The life-work and the life-struggle of many men are determined, doubtless, by unselfish and ideal motives, but to a far greater extent the less noble passions—craving for possessions, enjoyment and honour, envy and the thirst for revenge—determine men's actions. Still more often, perhaps, it is the need to live which brings down even natures of a higher mould into the universal struggle for existence and enjoyment. . . .

Now, it is, of course, an obvious fact that a peaceful rivalry may exist between peoples and States, like that between the fellow-members of a society, in all departments of civilized life—a struggle which need not always degenerate into war. Struggle and war are not identical. This rivalry, however, does not take place under the same conditions as the intrasocial struggle, and therefore cannot lead to the same results. Above the rivalry of individuals and groups within the State stands the law, which takes care that injustice is kept within bounds, and that the right shall prevail. Behind the law stands the State, armed with power, which it employs, and rightly so, not merely to protect, but actively to promote, the moral and spiritual interests of society. But there is no impartial power that stands above the rivalry of States to restrain injustice, and to use that rivalry with conscious purpose to promote the highest ends of mankind. Between States the only check on injustice is force, and in morality and civilization each people must play its own part and promote its own ends and ideals. If in doing so it comes into conflict with the ideals and views of other States, it must either submit and concede the precedence to the rival people or State, or appeal to force, and face the risk of the real struggle—i.e., of war—in order to make its own views prevail. No power exists which can judge between States, and makes its judgments prevail. Nothing, in fact, is left but war to secure to the true elements of progress the ascendancy over the spirits of corruption and decay.

It will, of course, happen that several weak nations unite and form a superior combination in order to defeat a nation which in itself is stronger. This attempt will succeed for a time, but in the end the more intensive vitality will prevail. The allied opponents have the seeds of corruption in them, while the powerful nation gains from a temporary reverse a new strength which procures for it an ultimate victory over numerical superiority. The history of Germany is an eloquent example of this truth.

Struggle is, therefore, a universal law of Nature, and the instinct of self-preservation which leads to struggle is acknowledged to be a natural condition of existence. "Man is a fighter." Self-sacrifice is a renunciation of life, whether in the existence of the individual or in the life of States, which are agglomerations of individuals. The first and paramount law is the assertion of one's own independent existence. By self-assertion alone can the State maintain the conditions of life for its citizens, and insure them the legal protection which each man is entitled to claim from it. This duty of self-assertion is by no means satisfied by the mere repulse of hostile attacks; it includes the obligation to assure the possibility of life and development to the whole body of the nation embraced by the State.

Strong, healthy, and flourishing nations increase in numbers. From a given moment they require a continual expansion of their frontiers, they require new territory for the accommodation of their surplus population. Since almost every part of the globe is inhabited, new territory must, as a rule, be obtained at the cost of its possessors—that is to say, by conquest, which thus becomes a law of necessity.

The right of conquest is universally acknowledged. At first the procedure is pacific. Overpopulated countries pour a stream of emigrants into other States and territories. These submit to the legislature of the new country, but try to obtain favourable conditions of existence for themselves at the cost of the original inhabitants, with whom they compete. This amounts to conquest.

The right of colonization is also recognized. Vast territories inhabited by uncivilized masses are occupied by more highly civilized States, and made subject to their rule. Higher civilization and the correspondingly greater power are the foundations of the right to annexation. This right is, it is true, a very indefinite one, and it is impossible to determine what degree of civilization justifies annexation and subjugation. The impossibility of finding a legitimate limit to these international relations has been the cause of many wars. The subjugated nation does not recognize this right of subjugation, and the more powerful civilized nation refuses to admit the claim of the subjugated to independence. This situation becomes peculiarly critical when the conditions of civilization have changed in the course of time. The subject nation has, perhaps, adopted higher methods and conceptions of life, and the difference in civilization has consequently lessened. Such a state of things is growing ripe in British India.

Lastly, in all times the right of conquest by war has been admitted. It may be that a growing people cannot win colonies from uncivilized races, and yet the State wishes to retain the surplus population which the mother-country can no longer feed. Then the only course left is to acquire the necessary territory by war. Thus the instinct of self-preservation leads inevitably to war, and the conquest of foreign soil. It is not the possessor, but the victor, who then has the right. . . .

In such cases might gives the right to occupy or to conquer. Might is at once the supreme right, and the dispute as to what is right is decided by the arbitrament of war. War gives a biologically just decision, since its decisions rest on the very nature of things. . . .

If we regard the life of the individual or of the nation as something purely material, as an incident which terminates in death and outward decay, we must logically consider that the highest goal which man can attain is the enjoyment of the most happy life and the greatest possible diminution of all bodily suffering. The State will be regarded as a sort of assurance office, which guarantees a life of undisturbed possession and enjoyment in the widest meaning of the word. We must endorse the view which Wilhelm von Humboldt professed in his treatise on the limits of the activity of the State.[35] The compulsory functions of the State must be limited to the assurance of property and life. The State will be considered as a law-court, and the individual will be inclined to shun war as the greatest conceivable evil.

If, on the contrary, we consider the life of men and of States as merely a fraction of a collective existence, whose final purpose does not rest on enjoyment, but on the development of intellectual and moral powers, and if we look upon all enjoyment merely as an accessory of the chequered conditions of life, the task of the State will appear in a very different light. The State will not be to us merely a legal and social insurance office, political union will not seem to us to have the one object of bringing the advantages of civilization within the reach of the individual; we shall assign to it the nobler task of raising the intellectual and moral powers of a nation to the highest expansion, and of securing for them that influence on the world which tends to the combined progress of humanity. We shall see in the State, as Fichte taught, an exponent of liberty to the human race, whose task it is to put into practice the moral duty on earth. "The State," says Treitschke, "is a moral community. It is called upon to educate the human race by positive achievement, and its ultimate object is that a nation should develop in it and through it into a real character; that is, alike for nation and individuals, the highest moral task."

This highest expansion can never be realized in pure individualism. Man can only develop his highest capacities when he takes his part in a community, in a social organism, for which he lives

35. D. W. von Humboldt, "Ideen zu einem Versuch, die Grenzen der Wirksamkelt des Staates zu bestimmen" [Ideas for an attempt to determine the limits of the effectiveness of the State].

and works. He must be in a family, in a society, in the State, which draws the individual out of the narrow circles in which he otherwise would pass his life, and makes him a worker in the great common interests of humanity. The State alone, so Schleiermacher once taught, gives the individual the highest degree of life.[36]

War, from this standpoint, will be regarded as a moral necessity, if it is waged to protect the highest and most valuable interests of a nation. As human life is now constituted, it is political idealism which calls for war, while materialism—in theory, at least—repudiates it.

If we grasp the conception of the State from this higher aspect, we shall soon see that it cannot attain its great moral ends unless its political power increases. The higher object at which it aims is closely correlated to the advancement of its material interests. It is only the State which strives after an enlarged sphere of influence that creates the conditions under which mankind develops into the most splendid perfection. The development of all the best human capabilities and qualities can only find scope on the great stage of action which power creates. But when the State renounces all extension of power, and recoils from every war which is necessary for its expansion; when it is content to exist, and no longer wishes to grow; when "at peace on sluggard's couch it lies," then its citizens become stunted. The efforts of each individual are cramped, and the broad aspect of things is lost. This is sufficiently exemplified by the pitiable existence of all small States, and every great Power that mistrusts itself falls victim to the same curse.

36. Bernhardi note: To expand the idea of the State into that of humanity, and thus to entrust apparently higher duties to the individual, leads to error, since in a human race conceived as a whole struggle and, by Implication, the most essential vital principle would be ruled out. Any action in favour of collective humanity outside the limits of the State and nationality is impossible. Such conceptions belong to the wide domain of Utopias.

All petty and personal interests force their way to the front during a long period of peace. Selfishness and intrigue run riot, and luxury obliterates idealism. Money acquires an excessive and unjustifiable power, and character does not obtain due respect. . . .

War, in opposition to peace, does more to arouse national life and to expand national power than any other means known to history. It certainly brings much material and mental distress in its train, but at the same time it evokes the noblest activities of the human nature. This is especially so under present-day conditions, when it can be regarded not merely as the affair of Sovereigns and Governments, but as the expression of the united will of a whole nation.

All petty private interests shrink into insignificance before the grave decision which a war involves. The common danger unites all in a common effort, and the man who shirks this duty to the community is deservedly spurned. This union contains a liberating power which produces happy and permanent results in the national life. We need only recall the uniting power of the War of Liberation[37] or the Franco-German War[38] and their historical consequences. The brutal incidents inseparable from every war vanish completely before the idealism of the main result. All the sham reputations which a long spell of peace undoubtedly fosters are unmasked. Great personalities take their proper place; strength, truth, and honour come to the front and are put into play. . . .

The individual can perform no nobler moral action than to pledge his life on his convictions, and to devote his own existence to the cause which he serves, or even to the conception of the value of ideals to personal morality. Similarly, nations and States can achieve no loftier consum-

37. The wars of the German states against Napoleon in 1813–14, in which French forces were driven from Central Europe.

38. Of 1870–71.

mation than to stake their whole power on up-holding their independence, their honour, and their reputation.

Such sentiments, however, can only be put into practice in war. The possibility of war is required to give the national character that stimulus from which these sentiments spring, and thus only are nations enabled to do justice to the highest duties of civilization by the fullest development of their moral forces. An intellectual and vigorous nation can experience no worse destiny than to be lulled into a Phaecian[39] existence by the undisputed enjoyment of peace.

From this point of view, efforts to secure peace are extraordinarily detrimental to the national health so soon as they influence politics. The States which from various considerations are always active in this direction are sapping the roots of their own strength. The United States of America, e.g., in June, 1911, championed the ideas of universal peace in order to be able to devote their undisturbed attention to money-making and the enjoyment of wealth, and to save the three hundred million dollars which they spend on their army and navy; they thus incur a great danger, not so much from the possibility of a war with England or Japan, but precisely because they try to exclude all chance of contest with opponents of their own strength, and thus avoid the stress of great political emotions, without which the moral development of the national character is impossible. If they advance farther on this road, they will one day pay dearly for such a policy.

Again, from the Christian standpoint we arrive at the same conclusion. Christian morality is based, indeed, on the law of love. "Love God above all things, and thy neighbour as thyself." This law can claim no significance for the relations of one country to another, since its application to politics would lead to a conflict of duties. The love which a

man showed to another country as such would imply a want of love for his own countrymen. Such a system of politics must inevitably lead men astray. Christian morality is personal and social, and in its nature cannot be political. Its object is to promote morality of the individual, in order to strengthen him to work unselfishly in the interests of the community. It tells us to love our individual enemies, but does not remove the conception of enmity. Christ Himself said: "I am not come to send peace on earth, but a sword." His teaching can never be adduced as an argument against the universal law of struggle. There never was a religion which was more combative than Christianity. Combat, moral combat, is its very essence. If we transfer the ideas of Christianity to the sphere of politics, we can claim to raise the power of the State—power in the widest sense, not merely from the material aspect—to the highest degree, with the object of the moral advancement of humanity, and under certain conditions the sacrifice may be made which a war demands. Thus, according to Christianity, we cannot disapprove of war in itself, but must admit that it is justified morally and historically.

Again, we should not be entitled to assume that from the opposite, the purely materialistic, standpoint war is entirely precluded. The individual who holds such views will certainly regard it with disfavour, since it may cost him life and prosperity. The State, however, as such can also come from the materialistic standpoint to a decision to wage war, if it believes that by a certain sacrifice of human lives and happiness the conditions of life of the community may be improved.

The loss is restricted to comparatively few, and, since the fundamental notion of all materialistic philosophy inevitably leads to selfishness, the majority of the citizens have no reason for not sacrificing the minority in their own interests. Thus, those who from the materialistic standpoint deny the necessity of war will admit its expediency from motives of self-interest.

39. In Homer's *The Odyssey*, this was the name given to the inhabitants of Scheria (modern-day Corfu), who were known for their hedonism.

Reflection thus shows not only that war is an unqualified necessity, but that it is justifiable from every point of view. . . .

With the cessation of the unrestricted competition, whose ultimate appeal is to arms, all real progress would soon be checked, and a moral and intellectual stagnation would ensue which must end in degeneration. So, too, when men lose the capacity of gladly sacrificing the highest material blessings—life, health, property, and comfort—for ideals; for the maintenance of national character and political independence; for the expansion of sovereignty and territory in the interests of the national welfare; for a definite influence in the concert of nations according to the scale of their importance in civilization; for intellectual freedom from dogmatic and political compulsion; for the honour of the flag as typical of their own worth—then progressive development is broken off, decadence is inevitable, and ruin at home and abroad is only a question of time. History speaks with no uncertain voice on this subject. It shows that valour is a necessary condition of progress. Where with growing civilization and increasing material prosperity war ceases, military efficiency diminishes, and the resolution to maintain independence under all circumstances fails, there the nations are approaching their downfall, and cannot hold their own politically or racially. . . .

These efforts for peace would, if they attained their goal, not merely lead to general degeneration, as happens everywhere in Nature where the struggle for existence is eliminated, but they have a direct damaging and unnerving effect. The apostles of peace draw large sections of a nation into the spell of their Utopian efforts, and they thus introduce an element of weakness into the national life; they cripple the justifiable national pride in independence, and support a nerveless opportunist policy by surrounding it with the glamour of a higher humanity, and by offering it specious reasons for disguising its own weakness. They thus play the game of their less scrupulous enemies, just as the Prussian policy, steeped in the ideas of universal peace, did in 1805 and 1806, and brought the State to the brink of destruction. . . .

Source: Friedrich von Bernhardi, Germany and the Next War, *http://www.fullbooks.com/Germany-and -the-Next-War1.html, accessed November 19, 2019.*

Supplementary Documents

At the Congress of Vienna in 1814–15, delegates recognized a Kingdom of the Netherlands, encompassing what is today the Netherlands and Belgium. However, the union between the two was not a happy one, with the northern part of the country Dutch speaking and Protestant and the southern part French speaking and Catholic. In 1830 the Belgians revolted and quickly secured support from neighboring France. An international conference was held in 1838 that recognized Belgian independence, and in 1839 Great Britain, France, Prussia, Austria, and Russia concluded the Treaty of London, in which Belgium was declared "perpetually neutral."

In 1870, when war broke out between Prussia and its allies (the North German Confederation) and France, both sides signed treaties with Great Britain reaffirming their pledges to respect the territorial integrity of Belgium.

Any violation of Belgian neutrality that may occur in the game would represent a violation of these treaties.

Quintuple Treaty signed by the European Powers at London, 1839

In the Name of the Most Holy and Indivisible Trinity.

Her Majesty the Queen of the United Kingdom of Great Britain and Ireland, His Majesty the Emperor of Austria, King of Hungary and Bohemia, His Majesty the King of the French, His Majesty the King of Prussia, and His Majesty the Emperor of all the Russias, having taken into consideration their Treaty concluded with His Majesty the King of the Belgians, on the 15th of November 1831; and His Majesty the King of the Netherlands, Grand Duke of Luxembourg, being disposed to conclude a definite arrangement on the basis of the 24 Articles agreed upon by the Plenipotentiaries of Great Britain, Austria, France, Prussia, and Russia on the 14th of October, 1831 . . .

Who, after having communicated to each other their Full Powers, found in good and due form, have agreed upon the following Articles:

ARTICLE 1

His Majesty the King of the Netherlands, Grand Duke of Luxembourg, engages to cause to be immediately converted into a Treaty with His Majesty the King of the Belgians, the Articles annexed to the present Act, and agreed upon by common consent, under the auspices of the Courts of Great Britain, Austria, France, Prussia and Russia. . . .

ARTICLE 3

The union which has existed between Holland and Belgium, in virtue of the Treaty of Vienna, of the 31st of May, 1815, is acknowledged by His Majesty the King of the Netherlands, Grand Duke of Luxembourg, to be dissolved. . . .

Done at London, the nineteenth day of April, in the year of Our Lord one thousand eight hundred and thirty-nine.

Annex to the Treaty signed at London, on the 19th of April, 1839, between Great Britain, Austria, France, Prussia and Russia, on the one part, and the Netherlands, on the Other. . . .

ARTICLE 7

Belgium . . . shall form an independent and perpetually neutral State. It shall be bound to observe such neutrality toward all other States.

Treaty signed between Great Britain and Prussia, 1870

Her Majesty the Queen of the United Kingdom of Great Britain and Ireland, and His Majesty the King of Prussia, being desirous at the present time of recording in a solemn Act their fixed determination to maintain the independence and neutrality of Belgium, as provided in Article 7 of the Treaty signed at London on the 19th of April, 1839, between Belgium and the Netherlands, which Article was declared by the Quintuple Treaty of 1839 to be considered as having the same force and value as if textually inserted in the said Quintuple Treaty, their said Majesties have determined to conclude between themselves a separate Treaty, which, without impairing or invalidating the conditions of the said Quintuple Treaty, shall be subsidiary and accessory to it. . . .

Who, after having communicated to each other their respective full powers, found in good and due form, have agreed upon and concluded the following Articles:

ARTICLE 1

His Majesty the King of Prussia having declared that, notwithstanding the hostilities in which the North German Confederation is engaged with France, it is his fixed determination to respect the neutrality of Belgium, so long as the same shall be respected by France, Her Majesty the Queen of the United Kingdom of Great Britain and Ireland on her part declares that, if during the said hostilities the armies of France should violate that neutrality, she will be prepared to co-operate with His Prussian Majesty for the defense of the same in such manner as may be mutually agreed upon, employing for that purpose her naval and military forces to insure its observance, and to maintain, in conjunction with His Prussian Majesty, then and thereafter, the independence and neutrality of Belgium.

It is clearly understood that Her Majesty the Queen of the United Kingdom of Great Britain and Ireland does not engage herself by this Treaty to take part in any of the general operations of the war now carried on between the North German Confederation and France, beyond the limits of Belgium, as defined in the Treaty between Belgium and the Netherlands of April 19, 1839.

ARTICLE 2

His Majesty the King of Prussia agrees on his part, in the event provided for in the foregoing Article, to co-operate with Her Majesty the Queen of the United Kingdom of Great Britain and Ireland, employing his naval and military forces for the purpose aforesaid; and, the case arising, to concert with Her Majesty the measures which shall be taken, separately or in common, to secure the neutrality and independence of Belgium.

ARTICLE 3

This Treaty shall be binding on the High Contracting Parties during the continuance of the present war between the North German Confederation and France, and for twelve months after the ratification of any Treaty of Peace concluded between those Parties; and on the expiration of that time the independence and neutrality of Belgium will, so far as the High Contracting Parties are respectively concerned, continue to rest as heretofore on Article 1 of the Quintuple Treaty of the 19th of April, 1839.

ARTICLE 4

The present Treaty shall be ratified, and the ratifications shall be exchanged at London as soon as possible.

In witness wherof the respective Plenipotentiaries have signed the same, and have affixed thereto the seal of their arms.

Done at London, the 9th day of August, in the year of our Lord 1870.

Treaty signed between Great Britain and France, 1870

Her Majesty the Queen of the United Kingdom of Great Britain and Ireland, and His Majesty the Emperor of the French, being desirous at the present time of recording in a solemn Act their fixed determination to maintain the independence and neutrality of Belgium, as provided by Article 7 of the Treaty signed at London on the 19th of April, 1839, between Belgium and the Netherlands, which Article was declared by the Quintuple Treaty of 1839 to be considered as having the same force and value as if textually in the said Quintuple Treaty, their said Majesties have determined to conclude between themselves a separate Treaty, which, without impairing or invalidating the conditions of the said Quintuple Treaty, shall be subsidiary and accessory to it. . . .

Who, after having communicated to each other their respective full powers, found in good and due form, have agreed upon and concluded the following Articles:

ARTICLE 1

His Majesty the Emperor of the French having declared that, notwithstanding the hostilities in which France is now engaged with the North German Confederation and its Allies, it is his fixed determination to respect the neutrality of Belgium, so long as the same shall be respected by the North German Confederation and its Allies, Her Majesty the Queen of the United Kingdom of Great Britain and Ireland on her part declares that, if during the said hostilities the armies of the North German Confederation and its Allies should violate that neutrality, she will be prepared to co-operate with His Imperial Majesty for the defense of the same in such manner as may be mutually agreed upon, employing for that purpose her naval and military forces to insure its observance, and to maintain, in conjunction with His Imperial Majesty, then and thereafter, the independence and neutrality of Belgium.

It is clearly understood that Her Majesty the Queen of the United Kingdom of Great Britain and Ireland does not engage herself by this Treaty to take part in any of the general operations of the war now carried on between France and the North German Confederation and its Allies, beyond the limits of Belgium, as defined in the Treaty between Belgium and the Netherlands of April 19, 1839.

ARTICLE 2

His Majesty the Emperor of the French agrees on his part, in the event provided for in the foregoing Article, to co-operate with Her Majesty the Queen of the United Kingdom of Great Britain and Ireland, employing his naval and military forces for the purpose aforesaid; and, the case arising, to concert with Her Majesty the measures which shall be taken, separately or in common, to secure the neutrality and independence of Belgium.

ARTICLE 3

This Treaty shall be binding on the High Contracting Parties during the continuance of the present war between France and the North German Confederation and its Allies, and for twelve months after the ratification of any Treaty of Peace concluded between those Parties; and on the expiration of that time the independence and neutrality Of Belgium will, so far as the High Contracting Parties are respectively concerned, continue to rest, as heretofore, on Article 1 of the Quintuple Treaty of the 19th of April, 1839.

ARTICLE 4

The present Treaty shall be ratified, and the ratifications shall be exchanged at London as soon as possible.

In witness whereof the respect[ive] Plenipotentiaries have signed the same, and have affixed thereto the seal of their arms.

Done at London, the 11th day of August, in the year of our Lord, 1870.

(L. S.) GRANVILLE
[British Foreign Secretary],

(L. S.) LA VALETTE
[French Minister of Foreign Affairs].

Source: Treaties and Documents Relative to the Neutrality of the Netherlands and Belgium, World

War I Document Archive, https://wwi.lib.byu.edu /index.php/Treaties_and_Documents_Relative_to _the_Neutrality_of_the_Netherlands_and_Belgium, accessed November 19, 2019.

EXCERPTS FROM A SPEECH BY GERMAN CHANCELLOR BERNHARD VON BÜLOW (1899)

After bringing about the unification of Germany, Chancellor Otto von Bismarck steered a conservative course in foreign policy. He worried that other states, fearful of German power on the continent, might form a coalition against Germany if the Reich behaved too forcefully on the world stage. However, Bismarck resigned in 1890 over a difference of opinion with Kaiser Wilhelm II, and thereafter the German government pursued a policy of Weltpolitik—"world policy"— aimed at building a large overseas empire and a modern navy. Bernhard von Bülow, who served as minister of state for foreign affairs from 1897 until 1900, and then as chancellor from 1900 to 1909, argues forcefully in this speech before the Reichstag that Germany must take its place among the colonial powers. His claim that Germany in the twentieth century would become "a hammer or an anvil" would prove eerily prophetic. Anyone seeking evidence of Germany's aggressive approach to foreign affairs will find plenty in this speech.

In our nineteenth century, England has increased its colonial empire—the largest the world has seen since the days of the Romans—further and further; the French have put down roots in North Africa and East Africa and created for themselves a new empire in the Far East; Russia has begun its mighty course of victory in Asia, leading it to the high plateau of the Pamir and to the coasts of the Pacific Ocean. Four years ago the Sino-Japanese war, [and] scarcely one and a half years ago the Spanish-American War have put things further in motion; they've led to great, momentous, far-reaching decisions, shaken old empires, and added new and serious ferment. . . . The English prime minister said a long time ago that the strong states were getting stronger and

stronger and the weak ones weaker and weaker. . . . We don't want to step on the toes of any foreign power, but at the same time we don't want our own feet tramped by any foreign power *(Bravo!)* and we don't intend to be shoved aside by any foreign power, not in political nor in economic terms. *(Lively applause.)* It is time, high time, that we . . . make it clear in our own minds what stance we have to take and how we need to prepare ourselves in the face of the processes taking place around us which carry the seeds within them for the restructuring of power relationships for the unforeseeable future. To stand inactively to one side, as we have done so often in the past, either from native modesty *(Laughter)* or because we were completely absorbed in our own internal arguments or for doctrinaire reasons—to stand dreamily to one side while other people split up the pie, we cannot and we will not do that. *(Applause.)* We cannot for the simple reason that we now have interests in all parts of the world. . . . The rapid growth of our population, the unprecedented blossoming of our industries, the hard work of our merchants, in short the mighty vitality of the German people have woven us into the world economy and pulled us into international politics. If the English speak of a "Greater Britain"; if the French speak of a "Nouvelle France"; if the Russians open up Asia; then we, too, have the right to a greater Germany *(Bravo! from the right, laughter from the left)*, not in the sense of conquest, but indeed in the sense of peaceful extension of our trade and its infrastructures. . . . We cannot and will not permit that the order of the day passes over the German people. . . . There is a lot of envy present in the world against us *(calls from the left)*, political envy and economic envy. There are individuals and there are interest groups, and there are movements, and there are perhaps even peoples that believe that the German was easier to have around and that the German was more pleasant for his neighbors in those earlier days, when, in spite of our education and in spite of our culture, foreigners looked down on us in political and economic matters like cavaliers with their noses in the air looking down on the humble tutor. *(Very true!—Laughter.)* These times of political faintness and economic and political humility should never return. *(Lively Bravo.)* We don't ever again want to become, as Friedrich List put it, the "slaves of humanity." But we'll only be able to keep ourselves at the fore if we realize that there is no welfare for us without power, without a strong army and a strong fleet. *(Very true! from the right; objections from the left.)* The means, gentlemen, for a people of almost 60 million—dwelling in the middle of Europe and, at the same time, stretching its economic antennae out to all sides—to battle its way through in the struggle for existence without strong armaments on land and at sea, have not yet been found. *(Very true! from the right.)* In the coming century the German people will be a hammer or an anvil.

Source: Bülow's 'Hammer and Anvil' Speech before the Reichstag, World War I Document Archive, https://wwi.lib.byu.edu/index.php /B%C3%BClow%27s_%27Hammer_and_Anvil%27 _Speech_before_the_Reichstag_(The_English _Translation), accessed November 19, 2019.

A.B.C., "BRITISH FOREIGN POLICY" (1901)

[The following article appeared in the British journal National Review *in November 1901. It was published at a time when, thanks to the government's nineteenth-century policy of "splendid isolation," Great Britain had no friends on the European continent. The realignment of strategy proposed here led directly to the Anglo-French Entente of 1904 and the Anglo-Russian Entente of 1907. The authors of this article remained anonymous at the time, although it was later revealed that one of them was Sir Edward Grey. The article is a fine illustration of Grey's worries that Germany was becoming a threat to the European balance of power.]*

The events which have occurred in South Africa during the last few years cannot fail to produce consequences deeper and more far-reaching than the most penetrating observer of contemporary politics could have contemplated at the moment a too famous Raid provoked a no less famous telegram. . . . Great Britain does not require an immense army of the approved Continental type, but she does require a splendidly equipped and highly trained force, ready for transportation at short notice to any part of her over-sea Empire which may be menaced. The British Navy should be increased so as to enable us to meet any three Powers at sea in superior numbers. The naval policy and avowed hostility of Germany, to which even the British official world can no longer remain blind, will force us to keep on a war-footing in the North Sea a fleet as powerful and efficient as the Mediterranean or Channel Squadrons. . . .

The lesson which foreign countries may learn from our war in South Africa is one that in their own interest each of them would do well to take to heart. We desire to avoid swagger, which is said to be a British characteristic, and is probably in varying forms a characteristic of every great nation which believes in itself and its future; but to all interested in understanding the real strength of this nation the Boer War should serve as a useful warning. The prolonged and exasperating struggle has once more exhibited in an impressive manner the political stability of British institutions and the steadfast character of the British race. Reflecting men can see that the living generation of Englishmen have in no way degenerated from their forbears of a hundred years ago. In the earlier period there were two men who appreciated the inherent strength of this country: one was William Pitt,[1] while the other was Napoleon Bonaparte. Pitt knew the meaning of Trafalgar. The conversation which he had in his last days with the young general who was rapidly rising to fame and who was destined to become the great Duke of Wellington, shows that his prescient intellect grasped the fact that, in spite of Austerlitz, if England were only true to herself, Nelson's victory must inevitably drive Napoleon to a policy which would so exas-

1. Pitt was prime minister during the Napoleonic Wars.

perate other nations that they would ultimately turn upon him—Spain giving the signal. His vision was fulfilled; England remained true to herself, and the steadfastness of her people extorted a remarkable tribute from Napoleon to his victorious enemies before the close of his life at St. Helena: "Had I been in 1815 the choice of the English as I was of the French, I might have lost the battle of Waterloo without losing a vote in the Legislature or a soldier from my ranks." During the last two years it has been abundantly demonstrated that the Englishmen of to-day have the same grit as their grandfathers, and the quiet, self-possessed manner in which they have faced the ignorant execration, and the political animosity of the civilized world is calculated to cause unfriendly communities to pause. They have with quiet resolution supported the Ministry—whose half-hearted measures have not always made support easy—simply because it was carrying on a war, and thousands and tens of thousands of men in England who have all their lives been bitter opponents of the political party now in power, have acted with the single object of strengthening the hands of the Government. There have been hours of difficulty, and even of danger, when more than one foreign Power desired, and tentatively sought, to form a coalition against this country. It was the temper of the people of the British Empire backed by the Navy that stunned into sobriety the zealous malignity of those who were willing to wound, but afraid to strike. The details of these sinister intrigues are not only familiar to the British Foreign Office, but their existence is known to the intelligent public; and we must admit at the outset that such shortsighted and fatuous cabals have not rendered easier the task of those who believe that the interests of England lie in the direction of improved relations with certain foreign Powers with whom at present British relations are only "friendly" in the strictly diplomatic sense. . . .

Closely connected with the subject of inter-imperial relations is the policy which the British Empire should pursue as regards other nations and empires. We shall have to re-consider our position with regard to them one by one; for it must be owned that some of our Ministers seem to be living under the spell of a diplomacy which the wisest of them has declared to be "antiquated." We wish to see this wisdom translated into action. We believe it to be the desire of the nation that these old-time prejudices and superstitions should be abandoned. The condition of the world has greatly changed during the past century. At the time when the "pilot who weathered the storm"[2] was laid in his grave at the foot of his father's statue in Westminster Abbey, France was ahead of all European countries as regards population, for she numbered twenty-five million souls. When England entered upon her titanic struggle with Napoleon, the whole European population of the British Empire did not exceed fifteen millions, while the population of the United States was not much larger than that of Australia at the present moment. To-day we are living in an entirely new world, the development and progress of which is the topic of almost every leading article, so we need not descant upon it here. Perhaps the main fact which should impress itself upon Englishmen in considering the actual international outlook is not merely the extraordinary growth of Germany—who has achieved greatness by trampling on her neighbors—but the fact that this formidable community is becoming increasingly dependent on a foreign food supply, as well as on foreign supplies of raw and partially manufactured articles. This necessarily involves the development of Germany as a Sea Power, and it is a matter for every European State to ponder over. She is already stronger at sea than either France or Russia. It therefore affects them as well as England, though up to a certain point they may welcome it, because it is the cause of German hostility to England. No one has brought this hostility so graphically before the British nation as the present Chancellor of the German Empire, Count von Bülow. He loses few opportunities in his highly

2. That is, William Pitt.

flavored discourses in the Reichstag of displaying his contempt for Great Britain, though both before and after more than one of these public demonstrations, private assurances have been conveyed to the British Government that the speaker need not be taken seriously as he was merely "conciliating" German Anglophobes—usually of the Agrarian class to which he belongs. One of these utterances, however, stands by itself, and as it is quite incapable of being explained away, Count von Bülow has not attempted any explanation. In reply to an interpellation, he informed the Reichstag that the telegram sent by Kaiser Wilhelm to President Kruger in 1896 was not, as had been represented in this country, the offspring of an unpremeditated impulse of resentment against the Jameson Raid, but it was a deliberate effort to ascertain how far Germany could reckon on the support of France and Russia in forming an anti-British combination. The Chancellor owned that the effort had failed, presumably because our supposed enemies were unwilling to play into the hands of Germany; he explained that, in consequence, German foreign policy had necessarily to take another tack, since "isolation" had been demonstrated. We doubt whether history records in the relations between great Powers a more impudent avowal of a more unfriendly act. It is galling to Englishmen to reflect that Germany was rewarded for failing to raise Europe against us by an Anglo-German agreement securing to her the reversion to spacious territories to which she has no sort of claim, though they may have been in the Kaiser's capacious mind when he dispatched his telegram.

The official advocates of the Naval Bills which have been introduced into the Reichstag during the last three years have made no concealment as to the objective of the modern German navy, and that portion of the German press which takes its cue from the Government has told us in language impossible to misunderstand that Germany aspires to deprive us of our position on the ocean. "*Unsere*

Zukunft liegt auf dem Wasser";[3] such is the swelling phrase of the Kaiser; but, like all his rhetoric, there is serious purpose behind it. At the present time it is estimated that a substantial proportion of the food of the entire population of Germany is sea-borne. She is becoming transformed from an agricultural into an industrial community, and if the process continues for another quarter of a century, while remaining secured against actual starvation by her land frontiers, she will become no less dependent on the ocean highways for her prosperity than we are. Great Britain is therefore confronted with the development of a new sea power founded on the same economic basis as herself, and impelled by a desire to be supreme. But *l'ocean ne comporte qu'un seul maître*.[4] We have secured in the past the sovereignty of the seas, and our sceptre cannot be wrested from us without a desperate and bloody struggle. Germany will not be so insane as to attempt this task single-handed, at any rate for many years to come; and it is for other Powers to consider in the interval whether it is for their advantage to support her in a joint attack on England, in which, as is evident from recent revelations, President Faure clearly foresaw that the brunt of battle would fall upon others, while the lion's share of any plunder would fall to Germany. It is by no means improbable that such a coalition might be worsted. We have before now successfully faced the world in arms on the ocean; but on the unlikely hypothesis of our fleet being crushed, it may be as well for other nations to make up their minds what they might expect to gain if the German eagle replaced the Union Jack as the symbol of sea power.

We approach the delicate question of our relations with Russia with considerable diffidence, as the omniscient German press has declared at any time during the last twenty years that the interests of England and Russia are as irreconcil-

3. "Our future lies on the water," that is, the world's oceans.
4. "The ocean has only one master."

able as their hatred is hereditary. It can hardly be denied that the "honest broker" in Berlin has exploited this assumed antagonism with much skill and no little profit to himself, but it has yet to be pointed out what benefit has accrued to either of the traditional antagonists. There are grounds for asserting that this question has lately been asked in responsible quarters in Russia, and that to-day the Russian Government is less ready "to pull the chestnuts out of the fire," to use a favorite Teutonic metaphor, for Count von Bülow than she used to be for his illustrious predecessor, Prince Bismarck. On the other hand, the failure of the Russian Emperor to act on the amiable exhortations of the leading German journals by taking advantage of our preoccupations in South Africa has made an unmistakable impression on the public opinion of this country. The *National Zeitung*, one of Prince Bismarck's favored organs, kindly informed us on October 1, 1899: "If England gets into military difficulties in South Africa, if the war is protracted, or if it takes an unfavorable turn, Russia would not remain idle. The opportunity for Russian aggrandizement in Asia would be too tempting." Of all countries in the world the Power which would have most reason to rue the substitution of Germany for Great Britain as the mistress of the seas would be Russia. When Kaiser Wilhelm came on his fruitful visit to England in the autumn of 1899, which produced the "graceful concession" on our part of Samoa, prominent Englishmen, who were inquisitive as to the significance of the great naval movement then under way in Germany, received the comforting assurance that German naval armaments were exclusively directed against Russia, being intended for co-operation with England in the Far East and for the maintenance of German interests in the Near East. In a sense, the latter suggestion expresses a substantially accurate fact. If once the sea power of England were overthrown, Germany would be free to execute her hostile policy towards Russia, who is not less in her way than we are. There is an idea growing steadily amongst Germans that Germany should expand into an empire branching from the Bosporus to the Persian Gulf; thus would territories be secured enjoying an excellent climate, to which the surplus stream of German population, which now flows to the United States and to the British Empire, might be diverted, without being lost to the German flag. This is by no means a new idea; it is the revival of an old idea, and it means of course the supremacy of Germany in the Near East and the supersession of the Slav by the Teuton. Such is the objective of those ambitious dreamers known as the Pan-Germanic League, a body most tenderly regarded by the German Government, and it embodies a policy as antagonistic to Russia as the German naval program is hostile to England.

Whatever the effect of recent developments may have been upon Russia, the attitude of the German nation and the suspicious policy of the German Government has led a continually increasing number of Englishmen to inquire whether it would not be worthwhile for England and Russia to discuss their differences with the object of arriving at a working understanding, and, if possible, a comprehensive settlement? Very distinguished Russians have frequently expressed an earnest desire that their country should seek an entente with England. The late Emperor Alexander openly avowed his desire for such a settlement . . . , but after his death [he] became convinced that it was hopeless to try and do business with this country, owing to the influence of a certain school of English politicians whose unreasoning antagonism to Russia almost amounts to a monomania. We hasten to say, however, that the fault does not lie exclusively with England. A main difficulty which confronts us whenever the subject is broached is that the central Government of St. Petersburg appears to be unable or unwilling to control the action of its more distant agents. We have had several conspicuous examples recently in China, e.g., where Russian officers have treated the property of, or pledged to, British subjects in a most high-handed and intolerable manner, in defiance of repeated assurances given to our Ambassador at

St. Petersburg. In fact, these cases were so bad that we do not care to dwell upon them. . . . At the same time, we in England must remember, when we complain of such conduct on the part of Russian agents, that, bad as it is, it is not more perfidious than actions which our Government appears willing to tolerate when Germany is the culprit. . . .

The chief political obstacle to an Anglo-Russian understanding is, no doubt, due to the desire of Russia to come down to the Persian Gulf. If we are able to recognize and tolerate her ambition in that quarter our antagonism would come to an end, at least for a generation. This admittedly is a subject of great difficulty, and one not to be settled off-hand; but that is no reason, as the *Times* has lately pointed out, why statesmen should not be prepared to face it. It is clearly our interest, as it is our intention, to preserve intact the status quo in the Gulf unless we can come to an arrangement with Russia by which we get a quid pro quo. That status has been lately threatened by the Sultan of Turkey at Kuwait, the port at the head of the Gulf which the Germans are believed to have marked as their future naval base, and which is to be the southern terminus of the great trunk line which will cross Constantinople. The Sultan of Turkey lately made use of certain local disturbances between Mubarak, the Sheikh of Kuwait and the Emir of Najd in order to assert his sovereignty over the independent sheikhs of the coast, and he counted on vindicating his pretensions over the ruler of Kuwait, after that personage had been defeated by his enemies. Accordingly, the Sultan sent a corvette-full of troops to Kuwait. Mubarak immediately applied for British protection, and when the Turks appeared they found one of our gunboats in the port, and the British officer informed the Turkish commander of the expedition that his troops would not be allowed to land. There the matter stands for the present, but the whole incident is illustrative of the handiwork of Germany, who was undoubtedly egging on the Sultan. The attempt was mainly directed against the British policy of upholding the present situation in the Persian Gulf, but, if successful, it might have a very considerable bearing on the future interests of Russia. Is it not idle to argue that Germany has "claims" to a port on the Persian Gulf, while we are to regard the appearance of Russia in that part of the world as a casus belli? Some acknowledged authorities have held that the manifest anxiety of Russia to penetrate into Southern Persia and to secure a seaport is a subject to be carefully considered by England. . . .

Russian statesmen have to make up their minds whether, in the present condition of Russian industries, Russian agriculture, and Russian finance, a friendly understanding with England, which would relieve her anxieties in the Far East, and which might result in her being able to continue her Trans-Caucasian and Siberian railways to the shores of the Persian Gulf, and which, last but not least, might enable her to carry out her historic mission in the Balkans, is not worth a high price.

Whether our readers agree with the view propounded in this paper or not we do not think that those who adopt a purely negative attitude by denying the existence of any basis for an entente between the Russian and British Empires are entitled to be heard. If others have a positive policy opposed to that which we are setting forth, by all means let them produce it, and induce or compel the British Government to adopt it and execute it. But in the interval we venture to sketch in outline some suggestions for a comprehensive settlement between the two Powers with the object of demonstrating to the sceptics that at any rate the raw material for an Anglo-Russian agreement abounds—whatever may be the case as regards the goodwill and statesmanship requisite to evolve the finished article. We would invite the reader to note that these suggestions are calculated to compromise neither the relations between Russia and France nor those between Great Britain and Japan.

Proposed Anglo-Russian Understanding

The understanding would naturally fall under three different heads:

I. The Near East

With regard to the Near East the basis would be that whilst Russia abstained from any attempt to interfere with the status quo in Egypt, we should frankly recognize that the fulfillment of what Russia regards as her historic mission in the Balkan peninsula conflicts with no vital British interests, and that in Asiatic Turkey we should abstain from favoring the development of German schemes of expansion.

II. Persia and Central Asia

With regard to Persia and Central Asia, we might offer Russia our cooperation in the development of railway communication between the Caspian and the Persian Gulf; and in securing for her a commercial outlet on the Gulf in return for an undertaking on the part of Russia to respect the political status quo along the shores of the Gulf. . . .

The fact of Russia being a party to such an agreement would give France a guarantee that her interests would be taken into due consideration, while our participation would afford a natural safeguard to the commercial interests of the United States.

The effect of such an agreement, accompanied by the customary demonstrations in such cases, public declarations by the Sovereigns and their official representatives, and an exchange of visits by their respective fleets, would at once remove the danger of a sudden explosion, which must continue to hang over the whole world so long as the Far East remains the powder-magazine of international rivalries and conflicting interests which it is at present.

The natural consequence of this understanding would be that in the event of war between Germany and Russia, Great Britain would remain neutral, and in the event of war between Great Britain and Germany, Russia would remain neutral. Russia would no longer give cause for suspicion that she was instigating France to make war against us . . . , and Great Britain would cease to be suspected in St. Petersburg of encouraging Japa-

nese hostility to Russia. Japan, on her side, would be relieved of the menace of a possible rival against her of the Triple Alliance of 1895. . . .

If we are to revert, as some of us desire, to the policy of Canning and Palmerston, and energetically support the cause of civil and religious liberty and popular rights in Europe, the time may not be remote when we should lift up our voices on behalf of the Czechs of Bohemia. In so doing we shall be promoting the real interests of the Austrian Empire; the question has been so persistently misrepresented that Englishmen are only beginning to realize that the Slavs of Austria are not the disintegrating force within that country. But it is the German element enrolled under the banner of the Pan-Germanic League which threatens the existence of an empire which a great Czech writer has told us would have to be created if it did not exist.

To sum up, then, the general conclusions of this paper: . . . We are the only great European Power which covets no European territory, and it ought not to be beyond the resources of our statesmanship to profit by this unique feature in our position. . . . It is our earnest desire to meet, if possible, the wishes of Russia, particularly on the Persian Gulf; but this policy is only practicable if Russia realizes that our cooperation is at least as valuable to her as hers is to us. We may, perhaps, be allowed to interject in passing that the different methods and systems of government and political institutions in the two empires need not interfere with their cordial relations, as some Russians seem inclined to apprehend. . . . Englishmen are beginning to realize that their institutions, however suitable to this country, are quite unsuitable even to nations whose historical development is much more similar to that of England than is the history of Russia. The Empire of the Tsars, on its side, possesses interesting and characteristic institutions which it would be disastrous to impair, but which could not be transferred to other soils.

In seeking to close our prolonged contest with Russia, we are desirous of doing something which would be for the advantage of civilization, and, should it be effected, it would not be less welcome because it brought us back into friendly relations with France—a country whose history is closely interwoven with our own, and with which we share so many political sentiments. The French are perhaps the only nation which will make sacrifices and run risks for the sake of those who enjoy their friendship. They are capable of sentimental attachment as well as sentimental hatred. . . .

But earnestly as we advocate a particular policy there should be no misunderstanding as to our motives. We are not touting for alliances. We are prepared to entertain friendly overtures, and to enter alliances on suitable terms and for practical purposes; and for the realization of ideals beneficial to the world at large we think Great Britain should be prepared to make considerable though reasonable sacrifices. But the people of this country will no longer tolerate a policy of "graceful concessions," and will not permit any Ministry or any personage however exalted to adopt towards any Power the attitude which has been too long followed as regards Germany. If Russia wishes to come to us, we shall meet her cordially and at least half way. If, on the other hand, Russia and France, one or both of them, elect to combine with Germany in an attempt to wrest from us the sceptre of the seas and to replace our sovereignty by that of Germany, England will know how to meet them. The Navy Bill in Germany was carried through with the avowed object of creating a navy which "would be able to keep the North Sea clear." We have no intention of clearing out of the North Sea or out of any other sea. We seek no quarrel with any Power but if Germany thinks it her interest to force one upon us, we shall not shrink from the ordeal, even should she appear in the lists with France and Russia as her allies. Germans would however, do well to realize that if England is driven to it, England will strike home. Close to the foundations of the German Empire, which has hardly emerged from its artificial stage, there exists a powder magazine such as is to be found in no other country viz., Social Democracy. In the case of a conflict with Great Britain, misery would be caused to large classes of the German population, produced by the total collapse of subsidized industries; far-reaching commercial depression, financial collapse, and a defective food-supply might easily make that magazine explode.

Source: "The ABC Proposal for British Foreign Policy," The World War I Document Archive, http://wwi.lib.byu.edu/index.php/The_ABC_Proposal_for_British_Foreign_Policy, accessed November 19, 2019.

THE ENTENTE CORDIALE BETWEEN GREAT BRITAIN AND FRANCE (1904)

The British government's decision to abandon "splendid isolation" after the Boer War led directly to the conclusion of the Entente Cordiale in 1904. This was not an alliance, but merely a settlement of differences between the countries regarding Egypt and Morocco. Nevertheless, it was regarded in Berlin as a serious threat—a sign that the two countries would now cooperate to threaten Germany's own interests in Africa.

ARTICLE 1

His Britannic Majesty's Government declare that they have no intention of altering the political status of Egypt.

The Government of the French Republic, for their part, declare that they will not obstruct the action of Great Britain in that country. . . .

It is agreed that the post of Director-General of Antiquities in Egypt shall continue, as in the past, to be entrusted to a French savant.

The French schools in Egypt shall continue to enjoy the same liberty as in the past.

ARTICLE 2

The Government of the French Republic declare that they have no intention of altering the political status of Morocco.

His Britannic Majesty's Government, for their part, recognise that it appertains to France, more particularly as a Power whose dominions are conterminous for a great distance with those of Morocco, to preserve order in that country, and to provide assistance for the purpose of all administrative, economic, financial, and military reforms which it may require.

They declare that they will not obstruct the action taken by France for this purpose, provided that such action shall leave intact the rights which Great Britain, in virtue of treaties, conventions, and usage, enjoys in Morocco, including the right of coasting trade between the ports of Morocco, enjoyed by British vessels since 1901.

ARTICLE 3

His Britannic Majesty's Government for their part, will respect the rights which France, in virtue of treaties, conventions, and usage, enjoys in Egypt, including the right of coasting trade between Egyptian ports accorded to French vessels.

ARTICLE 4

The two Governments, being equally attached to the principle of commercial liberty both in Egypt and Morocco, declare that they will not, in those countries, countenance any inequality either in the imposition of customs duties or other taxes, or of railway transport charges. The trade of both nations with Morocco and with Egypt shall enjoy the same treatment in transit through the French and British possessions in Africa. An agreement between the two Governments shall settle the conditions of such transit and shall determine the points of entry.

This mutual engagement shall be binding for a period of thirty years. Unless this stipulation is expressly denounced at least one year in advance, the period shall be extended for five years at a time.

Nevertheless the Government of the French Republic reserve to themselves in Morocco, and His Britannic Majesty's Government reserve to themselves in Egypt, the right to see that the concessions for roads, railways, ports, etc., are only granted on such conditions as will maintain intact

the authority of the State over these great undertakings of public interest.

ARTICLE 5

His Britannic Majesty's Government declare that they will use their influence in order that the French officials now in the Egyptian service may not be placed under conditions less advantageous than those applying to the British officials in the service.

The Government of the French Republic, for their part, would make no objection to the application of analogous conditions to British officials now in the Moorish service.

ARTICLE 6

In order to ensure the free passage of the Suez Canal, His Britannic Majesty's Government declare that they adhere to the treaty of the 29th October, 1888, and that they agree to their being put in force. The free passage of the Canal being thus guaranteed, the execution of the last sentence of paragraph 1 as well as of paragraph 2 of Article 8 of that treaty will remain in abeyance.

ARTICLE 7

In order to secure the free passage of the Straits of Gibraltar, the two Governments agree not to permit the erection of any fortifications or strategic works on that portion of the coast of Morocco comprised between, but not including, Melilla and the heights which command the right bank of the River Sebou.

This condition does not, however, apply to the places at present in the occupation of Spain on the Moorish coast of the Mediterranean.

ARTICLE 8

The two Governments, inspired by their feeling of sincere friendship for Spain, take into special consideration the interests which that country derives from her geographical position and from her territorial possessions on the Moorish coast of the Mediterranean. In regard to these interests the French Government will come to an understanding with the Spanish Government. The agreement which may be come to on the subject between France and Spain shall be communicated to His Britannic Majesty's Government.

ARTICLE 9

The two Governments agree to afford to one another their diplomatic support, in order to obtain the execution of the clauses of the present Declaration regarding Egypt and Morocco.

In witness whereof his Excellency the Ambassador of the French Republic at the Court of His Majesty the King of the United Kingdom of Great Britain and Ireland and of the British Dominions beyond the Seas, Emperor of India, and His Majesty's Principal Secretary of State for Foreign Affairs, duly authorised for that purpose, have signed the present Declaration and have affixed thereto their seals.

Done at London, in duplicate, the 8th day of April, 1904.

(L.S.) LANSDOWNE
[British Secretary of State for Foreign Affairs]

(L.S.) PAUL CAMBON
[French Ambassador to Great Britain]

SECRET ARTICLES
ARTICLE 1

In the event of either Government finding themselves constrained, by the force of circumstances, to modify their policy in respect to Egypt or Morocco, the engagements which they have undertaken towards each other by Articles 4, 6, and 7 of the Declaration of today's date would remain intact.

ARTICLE 2

His Britannic Majesty's Government have no present intention of proposing to the Powers any changes in the system of the Capitulations, or in the judicial organisation of Egypt.

In the event of their considering it desirable to introduce in Egypt reforms tending to assimilate the Egyptian legislative system to that in force in other civilised Countries, the Government of the French Republic will not refuse to entertain any such proposals, on the understanding that His Britannic Majesty's Government will agree to entertain the suggestions that the Government of the French Republic may have to make to them with a view of introducing similar reforms in Morocco.

ARTICLE 3

The two Governments agree that a certain extent of Moorish territory adjacent to Melilla, Ceuta, and other presides should, whenever the Sultan ceases to exercise authority over it, come within the sphere of influence of Spain, and that the administration of the coast from Melilla as far as, but not including, the heights on the right bank of the Sebou shall be entrusted to Spain.

Nevertheless, Spain would previously have to give her formal assent to the provisions of Articles 4 and 7 of the Declaration of today's date, and undertake to carry them out.

She would also have to undertake not to alienate the whole, or a part, of the territories placed under her authority or in her sphere of influence.

ARTICLE 4

If Spain, when invited to assent to the provisions of the preceding article, should think proper to decline, the arrangement between France and Great Britain, as embodied in the Declaration of today's date, would be none the less at once applicable.

ARTICLE 5

Should the consent of the other Powers to the draft Decree mentioned in Article 1 of the Declaration of today's date not be obtained, the Government of the French Republic will not oppose the repayment at par of the Guaranteed, Privileged, and Unified Debts after the 15th July, 1910.

Done at London, in duplicate, the 8th day of April, 1904.

(L.S.) LANSDOWNE

(L.S.) PAUL CAMBON

Source: *The Entente Cordiale Between England and France—April 8, 1904, The Avalon Project, https:// avalon.law.yale.edu/20th_century/entecord.asp, accessed November 20, 2019.*

THE ANGLO-RUSSIAN ENTENTE (1907)

Having settled its outstanding differences with France in the Entente Cordiale of 1904, the British government did the same with Russia three years later. The two countries had almost gone to war on several occasions in the nineteenth century, as British policymakers regarded Russian expansion in Central Asia as a threat to India. The Anglo-Russian Entente dealt entirely with Persia, which was divided into spheres of influence. Although this agreement was no more a formal alliance than was the Entente Cordiale, the kaiser's government interpreted the agreement as further evidence of a plot to "encircle" Germany and prevent it from becoming a world power.

Agreement Concerning Persia

The Governments of Great Britain and Russia having mutually engaged to respect the integrity and independence of Persia, and sincerely desiring the preservation of order throughout that country and its peaceful development, as well as the permanent establishment of equal advantages for the trade and industry of all other nations;

Considering that each of them has, for geographical and economic reasons, a special interest in the maintenance of peace and order in certain Provinces of Persia adjoining, or in the neighborhood of, the Russian frontier on the one hand, and the frontiers of Afghanistan and Baluchistan on the other hand; and being desirous of avoiding all cause of conflict between their respective interests in the above-mentioned Provinces of Persia;

Have agreed on the following terms:

I. Great Britain engages not to seek for herself, and not to support in favour of British subjects, or in favour of the subjects of third Powers, any Concessions of a political or commercial nature—such as Concessions for railways, banks, telegraphs, roads, transport, insurance, etc.—beyond a line starting from Kasr-i-Shirin, passing through Isfahan, Yezd, Kakhk, and ending at a point on the Persian frontier at the intersection of the Russian and Afghan frontiers, and not to oppose, directly or indirectly, demands for similar Concessions in this region which are supported by the Russian Government. It is understood that the above-mentioned places are included in the region in which Great Britain engages not to seek the Concessions referred to.

II. Russia, on her part, engages not to seek for herself and not to support, in favour of Russian subjects, or in favour of the subjects of third Powers, any Concessions of a political or commercial nature—such as Concessions for railways, banks, telegraphs, roads, transport, insurance, etc.—beyond a line going from the Afghan frontier by way of Gazik, Birjand, Kerman, and ending at Bunder Abbas, and not to oppose, directly or indirectly, demands for similar Concessions in this region which are supported by the British Government. It is understood that the above-mentioned places are included in the region in which Russia engages not to seek the Concessions referred to.

III. Russia, on her part, engages not to oppose, without previous arrangement with Great Britain, the grant of any Concessions whatever to British subjects in the regions of Persia situated between the lines mentioned in Articles 1 and 2.

Great Britain undertakes a similar engagement as regards the grant of Concessions to Russian subjects in the same regions of Persia. . . .

Source: *The Anglo-Russian Entente—1907, The Avalon Project, https://avalon.law.yale.edu/20th _century/angrusen.asp, accessed November 20, 2019.*

EXCERPTS FROM AN INTERVIEW WITH KAISER WILHELM II IN THE *LONDON DAILY TELEGRAPH* (1908)

Wilhelm II became kaiser of Germany in 1888. His grandmother had been the much-beloved Queen Victoria of Great Britain, and Wilhelm was a great admirer of the British Navy and the British Empire—so much so that he desired a similar navy and empire for his own country. The British government, however, regarded Germany's aggressive Weltpolitik of the 1890s and 1900s as a threat, and the kaiser himself as dangerously unstable. In 1908 a popular London newspaper, the Daily Telegraph, *ran an "interview" that was actually a set of notes made by a British army officer of conversations he had with Wilhelm in the previous year. The result was a major embarrassment for Germany, even leading to calls for the kaiser's abdication. This is a useful source for players seeking evidence of Germany's hostile attitude toward Great Britain.*

. . . "You English," he said, "are mad, mad, mad as March hares. What has come over you that you are so completely given over to suspicions quite unworthy of a great nation? What more can I do than I have done? I declared with all the emphasis at my command, in my speech at Guildhall, that my heart is set upon peace, and that it is one of my dearest wishes to live on the best of terms with England. Have I ever been false to my word? Falsehood and prevarication are alien to my nature. My actions ought to speak for themselves, but you listen not to them but to those who misinterpret and distort them. That is a personal insult which I feel and resent. To be forever misjudged, to have my repeated offers of friendship weighed and scrutinized with jealous, mistrustful eyes, taxes my patience severely. I have said time after time that I am a friend of England, and your press—, at least, a considerable section of it—bids the people of England refuse my proffered hand and insinuates that the other holds a dagger. How can I convince a nation against its will?

"I repeat," continued His Majesty, "that I am a friend of England, but you make things difficult for me. My task is not of the easiest. The prevailing sentiment among large sections of the middle and lower classes of my own people is not friendly to England. I am, therefore so to speak, in a minority in my own land, but it is a minority of the best elements as it is in England with respect to Germany. That is another reason why I resent your refusal to accept my pledged word that I am the friend of England. I strive without ceasing to improve relations, and you retort that I am your archenemy. You make it hard for me. Why is it?" . . .

His Majesty then reverted to the subject uppermost in his mind—his proved friendship for England. "I have referred," he said, "to the speeches in which I have done all that a sovereign can do to proclaim my good-will. But, as actions speak louder than words, let me also refer to my acts. It is commonly believed in England that throughout the South African War Germany was hostile to her. German opinion undoubtedly was hostile—bitterly hostile. But what of official Germany? Let my critics ask themselves what brought to a sudden stop, and, indeed, to absolute collapse, the European tour of the Boer delegates, who were striving to obtain European intervention? They were feted in Holland, France gave them a rapturous welcome. They wished to come to Berlin, where the German people would have crowned them with flowers. But when they asked me to receive them—I refused. The agitation immediately died away, and the delegation returned empty-handed. Was that, I ask, the action of a secret enemy?

"Again, when the struggle was at its height, the German government was invited by the governments of France and Russia to join with them in calling upon England to put an end to the war. The moment had come, they said, not only to save the Boer Republics, but also to humiliate England to the dust. What was my reply? I said that so far from Germany joining in any concerted European action to put pressure upon England and bring about her downfall, Germany would always keep aloof from politics that could bring her into complications with a sea power like England. Posterity will one day read the exact terms of the telegram—now in the archives of Windsor Castle—in which I informed the sovereign of England of the answer I had returned to the Powers which then sought to compass her fall. Englishmen who now insult me by doubting my word should know what were my actions in the hour of their adversity.

"Nor was that all. Just at the time of your Black Week, in the December of 1899, when disasters followed one another in rapid succession, I received a letter from Queen Victoria, my revered grandmother, written in sorrow and affliction, and bearing manifest traces of the anxieties which were preying upon her mind and health. I at once returned a sympathetic reply. Nay, I did more. I bade one of my officers procure for me as exact an account as he could obtain of the number of combatants in South Africa on both sides and of the actual position of the opposing forces. With the figures before me, I worked out what I considered the best plan of campaign under the circumstances, and submitted it to my General Staff for their criticism. Then, I dispatched it to England, and that document, likewise, is among the state papers at Windsor Castle, awaiting the severely impartial verdict of history. And, as a matter of curious coincidence, let me add that the plan which I formulated ran very much on the same lines as that which was actually adopted by Lord Roberts, and carried by him into successful operation. Was that, I repeat, an act of one who wished England ill? Let Englishmen be just and say!

"But, you will say, what of the German navy? Surely, that is a menace to England! Against whom but England are my squadrons being prepared? If England is not in the minds of those Germans who are bent on creating a powerful fleet, why is Germany asked to consent to such new and heavy burdens of taxation? My answer is clear. Germany is a young and growing empire. She has a world-wide commerce which is rapidly expanding, and to which the legitimate ambition of patriotic Germans refuses to assign any bounds. Germany must have a powerful fleet to protect that commerce and her manifold interests in even the most distant seas. She expects those interests to go on growing, and she must be able to champion them manfully in any quarter of the globe. Her horizons stretch far away." . . .

Source: Daily Telegraph. *London, October 28, 1908. Reprinted in Louis L. Snyder, ed.,* Documents of German History *(New Brunswick, NJ: Rutgers University Press, 1958), 296–300.*

EXCERPT FROM A SPEECH BY BRITISH CHANCELLOR OF THE EXCHEQUER DAVID LLOYD GEORGE (1911)

An international crisis erupted in July 1911 when, in protest against French attempts to establish control over Morocco, the German government chose to make a show of force by sending a gunboat to the Moroccan port of Agadir. Apparently, Berlin assumed that Great Britain would express disinterest and France would be forced to back down, thus driving a wedge between the powers of the newly concluded Triple Entente. However, the Germans were to be disappointed. In a speech at Mansion House, the official residence of the Lord Mayor of London, British chancellor of the exchequer David Lloyd George warned that Britain would fight for its "national honour." The address had special force, given that Lloyd George had a reputation for pacifism and hostility to imperialism, and soon afterward the German government backed down.

Personally I am a sincere advocate of all means which would lead to the settlement of international disputes by methods such as those which civilization has so successfully set up for the adjustment of differences between individuals, and I rejoice in my heart at the prospect of a happy issue to Sir Edward Grey's negotiations with the United States of America for the settlement of disputes which may occur in future between ourselves and our kinsmen across the Atlantic by some more merciful, more rational, and by a more just arbitrament than that of the sword.

But I am also bound to say this—that I believe it is essential in the highest interests, not merely of this country, but of the world, that Britain should at all hazards maintain her place and her prestige amongst the Great Powers of the world. Her potent influence has many a time been in the past, and may yet be in the future, invaluable to the cause of human liberty. It has more than once in the past redeemed Continental nations, who are sometimes too apt to forget that service, from overwhelming disaster and even from national extinction. I would make great sacrifices to preserve peace. I conceive that nothing would justify a disturbance of international good will except questions of the greatest national moment. But if a situation were to be forced upon us in which peace could only be preserved by the surrender of the great and beneficent position Britain has won by centuries of heroism and achievement, by allowing Britain to be treated where her interests were vitally affected as if she were of no account in the Cabinet of nations, then I say emphatically that peace at that price would be a humiliation in tolerable for a great country like ours to endure. National honour is no party question. The security of our great international trade is no party question; the peace of the world is much more likely to be secured if all nations realize fairly what the conditions of peace must be. . . .

Source: Lloyd George's Mansion House Speech, 21 July 1911, World War I Document Archive, https:// wwi.lib.byu.edu/index.php/Agadir_Crisis:_Lloyd _George%27s_Mansion_House_Speech, accessed November 19, 2019.

MANIFESTO OF THE NARODNA ODBRANA (1911)

The Austro-Hungarian annexation of Bosnia-Herzegovina in 1908 caused outrage among Serbian nationalists, who had expected that the province—mainly inhabited by Serbs—would become part of Serbia. The annexation led directly to the creation of the Narodna Odbrana *(Defence of the People), a secret patriotic society dedicated to rallying the Serbian people—both inside and outside Serbia—for an eventual fight against Austria-Hungary. This document, a pamphlet issued by the organization in 1911, should be of use to any player who seeks to demonstrate Serbian hostility toward Austria-Hungary.*

The annexation *[of Bosnia and Herzegovina]* was only one of the blows which the enemies of Serbia have aimed at this land. Many blows preceded it, and many will follow it. Work and preparation are necessary so that a new attack may not find Serbia equally unprepared.

The object assigned to the work to be done by the people of every class is the preparation for war in all forms of national work, corresponding to the requirements of the present day. This is to be effected through strengthening of the national consciousness, bodily exercises, increase of material and bodily well-being, cultural improvements, etc. A new blow, like that of the annexation, must be met by a new Serbia, in which every Serbian, from child to greybeard, is a rifleman.

The old Turks of the South gradually disappear and only a part of our people suffer under their rule. But new Turks come from the North, more fearful and dangerous than the old; stronger in civilization and more advanced economically, our northern enemies come against us. They want to take our freedom and our language from us and to crush us. We can already feel the presages of the struggle which approaches in that quarter. The Serbian people are faced by the question "to be or not to be?"

The Narodna Odbrana does not doubt that in the fight against the enemies with whom we stand face to face, our people will provide a succession of heroes. However, the Narodna Odbrana is not content with this, for it regards the so-called peaceful present-day conditions as war, and demands heroes, too, for this struggle of today which we are carrying on in Serbia and beyond the frontier.

In using the word "people" the Narodna Odbrana means our whole people, not only those in Serbia. It is hoped that the work done by it in Serbia will spur the brothers outside Serbia to take a more energetic share in the work of private initiative, so that the new present-day movement for the creation of a powerful Serbian Narodna Odbrana will go forward in unison in all Serbian territories.

The Narodna Odbrana proclaims to the people that Austria is our first and greatest enemy. Just as once the Turks attacked us from the south, so Austria attacks us today from the north. If the Narodna Odbrana preaches the necessity of fighting Austria, she preaches a sacred truth of our national position.

For the sake of bread and room, for the sake of the fundamental essentials of culture and trade, the freeing of the conquered Serbian territories and their union with Serbia is necessary to gentlemen, tradesmen, and peasants alike.

While the Narodna Odbrana works in conformity with the times according to the altered conditions, it also maintains all the connections made at the time of the annexation; today therefore it is the same as it was at the time of the annexation. Today, too, it is Odbrana (defense); today, too, Narodna (of the people); today, too, it gathers under its standard the citizens of Serbia as it gathered them at the time of the annexation. Then the cry was for war, now the cry is for work. Then meetings, demonstrations, voluntary clubs, weapons, and bombs were asked for; today steady, fanatical, tireless work and again work is required to fulfil the tasks and duties to which we have drawn attention by way of present preparation for the fight with gun and cannon which will come.

Source: The Narodna Odbrana, 1911, World War I Document Archive, https://wwi.lib.byu.edu/index .php/The_Narodna_Odbrana, accessed November 19, 2019.

EXCERPTS FROM CHAPTER V OF FRIEDRICH VON BERNHARDI, *GERMANY AND THE NEXT WAR* (1912)

In this excerpt from Germany and the Next War, *von Bernhardi considers Germany's position in the world. Players in the German faction will find this useful for explaining the threats Germany faces from England, France, and Russia. Members of other factions may point to this as more evidence that Germany bears aggressive intentions toward its neighbors.*

V. World Power or Downfall

In discussing the duties which fall to the German nation from its history and its general as well as particular endowments, we attempted to prove that a consolidation and expansion of our position among the Great Powers of Europe, and an extension of our colonial possessions, must be the basis of our future development.

The political questions thus raised intimately concern all international relations, and should be thoroughly weighed. We must not aim at the impossible. A reckless policy would be foreign to our national character and our high aims and duties. But we must aspire to the possible, even at the risk of war. This policy we have seen to be both our right and our duty. The longer we look at things with folded hands, the harder it will be to make up the start which the other Powers have gained on us. . . .

The sphere in which we can realize our ambition is circumscribed by the hostile intentions of the other World Powers, by the existing territorial conditions, and by the armed force which is at the back of both. Our policy must necessarily be determined by the consideration of these conditions. We must accurately, and without bias or timidity, examine the circumstances which turn the scale when the forces which concern us are weighed one against the other.

These considerations fall partly within the military, but belong mainly to the political sphere, in so far as the political grouping of the States allows a survey of the military resources of the parties. We must try to realize this grouping. The shifting aims of the politics of the day need not be our standard; they are often coloured by considerations of present expediency, and offer no firm basis for forming an opinion. We must rather endeavour to recognize the political views and intentions of the individual States, which are based on the nature of things, and therefore will continually make their importance felt. The broad lines of policy are ultimately laid down by the permanent interests of a country, although they may often be mistaken from short-sightedness or timidity, and although policy sometimes takes a course which does not seem warranted from the standpoint of lasting national benefits. Policy is not an exact science, following necessary laws, but is made by men who impress on it the stamp of their strength or their weakness, and often divert it from the path of true national interests. Such digressions must not be ignored. The statesman who seizes his opportunity will often profit by these political fluctuations. But the student who considers matters from the standpoint of history must keep his eyes mainly fixed on those interests which seem permanent. We must therefore try to make the international situation in this latter sense clear, so far as it concerns Germany's power and ambitions.

We see the European Great Powers divided into two great camps.

On the one side Germany, Austria, and Italy have concluded a defensive alliance, whose sole object is to guard against hostile aggression. In this alliance the two first-named States form the solid, probably unbreakable, core, since by the nature of things they are intimately connected. The geographical conditions force this result. The two States combined form a compact series of territories from the Adriatic to the North Sea and the Baltic. Their close union is due also to historical national and political conditions. Austrians have fought shoulder to shoulder with Prussians and Germans of the Empire on a hundred battlefields; Germans are the backbone of the Austrian dominions, the bond of union that holds together the different nationalities of the Empire. Austria, more than Germany, must guard against the inroads of Slavism, since numerous Slavonic [Slavic] races are comprised in her territories. There has been no conflict of interests between the two States since the struggle for the supremacy in Germany was decided. The maritime and commercial interests of the one point to the south and south-east, those of the other to the north. Any feebleness in the one must react detrimentally on the political relations of the other. A quarrel between Germany and Austria would leave both States at the mercy of overwhelmingly powerful enemies. The possibility of each maintaining its political position depends on their standing by each other. It may be assumed that the relations uniting the two States will be permanent so long as Germans and Magyars are the leading nationalities in the Danubian monarchy. It was one of the master-strokes of Bismarck's policy to have recognized the community of Austro-German interests even during the war of 1866, and boldly to have concluded a peace which rendered such an alliance possible.

The weakness of the Austrian Empire lies in the strong admixture of Slavonic [Slavic] elements, which are hostile to the German population, and show many signs of Pan-Slavism. It is not at present, however, strong enough to influence the political position of the Empire.

Italy, also, is bound to the Triple Alliance by her true interests. The antagonism to Austria, which has run through Italian history, will diminish when the needs of expansion in other spheres, and of creating a natural channel for the increasing population, are fully recognized by Italy. Neither condition is impossible. Irredentism will then lose its political significance, for the position, which belongs to Italy from her geographical situation and her past history, and will promote her true interests if attained, cannot be won in a war with Austria. It is the position of a leading political and commercial Mediterranean Power. That is the natural heritage which she can claim. Neither Germany nor Austria is a rival in this claim, but France, since she has taken up a permanent position on the coast of North Africa, and especially in Tunis, has appropriated a country which would have been the most natural colony for Italy, and has, in point of fact, been largely colonized by Italians. It would, in my opinion, have been politically right for us, even at the risk of a war with France, to protest against this annexation, and to preserve the territory of Carthage for Italy. We should have considerably strengthened Italy's position on the Mediterranean, and created a cause of contention between Italy and France that would have added to the security of the Triple Alliance.

The weakness of this alliance consists in its purely defensive character. It offers a certain security against hostile aggression, but does not consider the necessary development of events, and does not guarantee to any of its members help in the prosecution of its essential interests. It is based on a *status quo*, which was fully justified in its day, but has been left far behind by the march of political events. Prince Bismarck, in his "Thoughts and Reminiscences," pointed out that this alliance would not always correspond to the requirements of the future. Since Italy found the Triple Alliance did not aid her Mediterranean policy, she tried to effect a pacific agreement with England and France, and accordingly retired from the Triple Alliance. The results of this policy are manifest to-day. Italy, under an undisguised arrangement with England and France, but in direct opposition to the interests of the Triple Alliance, attacked Turkey, in order to conquer, in Tripoli, the required colonial territory. This undertaking brought her to the brink of a war with Austria, which, as the supreme Power in the Balkan Peninsula, can never tolerate the encroachment of Italy into those regions.

The Triple Alliance, which in itself represents a natural league, has suffered a rude shock. The ultimate reason for this result is found in the fact that the parties concerned with a narrow, short-sighted policy look only to their immediate private interests, and pay no regard to the vital needs of the members of the league. The alliance will not regain its original strength until, under the protection of the allied armies, each of the three States can satisfy its political needs. We must therefore be solicitous to promote Austria's position in the Balkans, and Italy's interests on the Mediterranean. Only then can we calculate on finding in our allies assistance towards realizing our own political endeavours. Since, however, it is against

all our interests to strengthen Italy at the cost of Turkey, which is, as we shall see, an essential member of the Triple Alliance, we must repair the errors of the past, and in the next great war win back Tunis for Italy. Only then will Bismarck's great conception of the Triple Alliance reveal its real meaning. But the Triple Alliance, so long as it only aims at negative results, and leaves it to the individual allies to pursue their vital interests exclusively by their own resources, will be smitten with sterility. On the surface, Italy's Mediterranean interests do not concern us closely. But their real importance for us is shown by the consideration that the withdrawal of Italy from the Triple Alliance, or, indeed, its secession to an Anglo-Franco-Russian *entente*, would probably be the signal for a great European war against us and Austria. Such a development would gravely prejudice the lasting interests of Italy, for she would forfeit her political independence by so doing, and incur the risk of sinking to a sort of vassal state of France. Such a contingency is not unthinkable, for, in judging the policy of Italy, we must not disregard her relations with England as well as with France.

England is clearly a hindrance in the way of Italy's justifiable efforts to win a prominent position in the Mediterranean. She possesses in Gibraltar, Malta, Cyprus, Egypt, and Aden a chain of strong bases, which secure the sea-route to India, and she has an unqualified interest in commanding this great road through the Mediterranean. England's Mediterranean fleet is correspondingly strong and would—especially in combination with the French Mediterranean squadron—seriously menace the coasts of Italy, should that country be entangled in a war against England *and* France. Italy is therefore obviously concerned in avoiding such a war, as long as the balance of maritime power is unchanged. She is thus in an extremely difficult double position; herself a member of the Triple Alliance, she is in a situation which compels her to make overtures to the opponents of that alliance, so long as her own allies can afford no trustworthy assistance to her policy of development. It is our interest to reconcile Italy and Turkey so far as we can.

France and Russia have united in opposition to the Central European Triple Alliance. France's European policy is overshadowed by the idea of *revanche*.[5] For that she makes the most painful sacrifices; for that she has forgotten the hundred years' enmity against England and the humiliation of Fashoda. She wishes first to take vengeance for the defeats of 1870–71, which wounded her national pride to the quick; she wishes to raise her political prestige by a victory over Germany, and, if possible, to regain that former supremacy on the continent of Europe which she so long and brilliantly maintained; she wishes, if fortune smiles on her arms, to reconquer Alsace and Lorraine. But she feels too weak for an attack on Germany. Her whole foreign policy, in spite of all protestations of peace, follows the single aim of gaining allies for this attack. Her alliance with Russia, her *entente* with England, are inspired with this spirit; her present intimate relations with this latter nation are traceable to the fact that the French policy hoped, and with good reason, for more active help from England's hostility to Germany than from Russia.

The colonial policy of France pursues primarily the object of acquiring a material, and, if possible, military superiority over Germany. The establishment of a native African army, the contemplated introduction of a modified system of conscription in Algeria, and the political annexation of Morocco, which offers excellent raw material for soldiers, so clearly exhibit this intention, that there can be no possible illusion as to its extent and meaning.

Since France has succeeded in bringing her military strength to approximately the same level as Germany, since she has acquired in her North African Empire the possibility of considerably increasing that strength, since she has completely outstripped Germany in the sphere of colonial policy, and has not only kept up, but also revived, the French sympathies of Alsace and Lorraine, the conclusion is obvious: France will not abandon the paths of an anti-German policy, but will do her best to excite hostility against us, and to thwart German interests in every quarter of the globe. When she came to an understanding with the Italians, that she should be given a free hand in Morocco if she allowed them to occupy Tripoli, a wedge was driven into the Triple Alliance which threatens to split it. It may be regarded as highly improbable that she will maintain honourably and with no *arrière-pensée*[6] the obligations undertaken in the interests of German commerce in Morocco. The suppression of these interests was, in fact, a marked feature of the French Morocco policy, which was conspicuously anti-German. The French policy was so successful that we shall have to reckon more than ever on the hostility of France in the future. It must be regarded as a quite unthinkable proposition that an agreement between France and Germany can be negotiated before the question between them has been once more decided by arms. Such an agreement is the less likely now that France sides with England, to whose interest it is to repress Germany but strengthen France. Another picture meets our eyes if we turn to the East, where the giant Russian Empire towers above all others.

The Empire of the Czar, in consequence of its defeat in Manchuria, and of the revolution which was precipitated by the disastrous war, is following apparently a policy of recuperation. It has tried to come to an understanding with Japan in the Far East, and with England in Central Asia; in the Balkans its policy aims at the maintenance of the *status quo*. So far it does not seem to have entertained any idea of war with Germany. The Potsdam agreement, whose importance cannot be overestimated, shows that we need not anticipate at present any aggressive policy on Russia's part. The

---

5. A policy of revenge, specifically aimed at recovering lost territories (in this case, Alsace-Lorraine).

6. Mental reservation.

ministry of Kokowzew[7] seems likely to wish to continue this policy of recuperation, and has the more reason for doing so, as the murder of Stolypin[8] with its accompanying events showed, as it were by a flash of lightning, a dreadful picture of internal disorder and revolutionary intrigue. It is improbable, therefore, that Russia would now be inclined to make armed intervention in favour of France. The Russo-French alliance is not, indeed, swept away, and there is no doubt that Russia would, if the necessity arose, meet her obligations; but the tension has been temporarily relaxed, and an improvement in the Russo-German relations has been effected, although this state of things was sufficiently well paid for by the concessions of Germany in North Persia.

It is quite obvious that this policy of marking time, which Russia is adopting for the moment, can only be transitory. The requirements of the mighty Empire irresistibly compel an expansion towards the sea, whether in the Far East, where it hopes to gain ice-free harbours, or in the direction of the Mediterranean, where the Crescent still glitters on the dome of St. Sophia. After a successful war, Russia would hardly hesitate to seize the mouth of the Vistula, at the possession of which she has long aimed, and thus to strengthen appreciably her position in the Baltic.

Supremacy in the Balkan Peninsula, free entrance into the Mediterranean, and a strong position on the Baltic, are the goals to which the European policy of Russia has naturally long been directed. She feels herself, also, the leading power of the Slavonic [Slavic] races, and has for many years been busy in encouraging and extending the spread of this element into Central Europe.

Pan-Slavism is still hard at work.

It is hard to foresee how soon Russia will come out from her retirement and again tread the natural paths of her international policy. Her present political attitude depends considerably on the person of the present Emperor, who believes in the need of leaning upon a strong monarchical State, such as Germany is, and also on the character of the internal development of the mighty Empire. The whole body of the nation is so tainted with revolutionary and moral infection, and the peasantry is plunged in such economic disorder, that it is difficult to see from what elements a vivifying force may spring up capable of restoring a healthy condition. Even the agrarian policy of the present Government has not produced any favourable results, and has so far disappointed expectations. The possibility thus has always existed that, under the stress of internal affairs, the foreign policy may be reversed and an attempt made to surmount the difficulties at home by successes abroad. Time and events will decide whether these successes will be sought in the Far East or in the West. On the one side Japan, and possibly China, must be encountered; on the other, Germany, Austria, and, possibly, Turkey.

Doubtless these conditions must exercise a decisive influence on the Franco-Russian Alliance. The interests of the two allies are not identical. While France aims solely at crushing Germany by an aggressive war, Russia from the first has more defensive schemes in view. She wished to secure herself against any interference by the Powers of Central Europe in the execution of her political plans in the South and East, and at the same time, at the price of an alliance, to raise, on advantageous terms in France, the loans which were so much needed. Russia at present has no inducement to seek an aggressive war with Germany or to take part in one. Of course, every further increase of the German power militates against the Russian interests. We shall therefore

7. Count Vladimir Nikolaevich Kokovtsov (1853–1943) was chairman of Russia's council of ministers from 1911 until his retirement at the end of January 1914. As prime minister he was the leading advocate of a cautious foreign policy, and he was thus despised by the pan-Slav activists at the tsar's court.

8. Pyotr Arkadyevich Stolypin (1862–1911) was Kokovtsov's predecessor as chairman of the council of ministers. He was assassinated in September 1911.

always find her on the side of those who try to cross our political paths.

England has recently associated herself with the Franco-Russian Alliance. She has made an arrangement in Asia with Russia by which the spheres of influence of the two parties are delimited, while with France she has come to terms in the clear intention of suppressing Germany under all circumstances, if necessary by force of arms.

The actually existing conflict of Russian and English interests in the heart of Asia can obviously not be terminated by such agreements. So, also, no natural community of interests exists between England and France. A strong French fleet may be as great a menace to England as to any other Power. For the present, however, we may reckon on an Anglo-French *entente*. This union is cemented by the common hostility to Germany. No other reason for the political combination of the two States is forthcoming. There is not even a credible pretext, which might mask the real objects.

This policy of England is, on superficial examination, not very comprehensible. Of course, German industries and trade have lately made astounding progress, and the German navy is growing to a strength which commands respect. We are certainly a hindrance to the plans which England is prosecuting in Asiatic Turkey and Central Africa. This may well be distasteful to the English from economic as well as political and military aspects. But, on the other hand, the American competition in the domain of commercial politics is far keener than the German. The American navy is at the present moment stronger than the German, and will henceforth maintain this precedence. Even the French are on the point of building a formidable fleet, and their colonial Empire, so far as territory is concerned, is immensely superior to ours. Yet, in spite of all these considerations, the hostility of the English is primarily directed against us. It is necessary to adopt the English standpoint in order to understand the line of thought which guides the English politicians. I believe that the solution of the

problem is to be found in the wide ramifications of English interests in every part of the world. . . .

Turkey is the only State which might seriously threaten the English position in Egypt by land. This contingency gives to the national movement in Egypt an importance which it would not otherwise possess; it clearly shows that England intensely fears every Pan-Islamitic movement. She is trying with all the resources of political intrigue to undermine the growing power of Turkey, which she officially pretends to support, and is endeavouring to create in Arabia a new religious centre in opposition to the Caliphate.

The same views are partially responsible for the policy in India, where some seventy millions of Moslems live under the English rule. England, so far, in accordance with the principle of *divide et impera*,[9] has attempted to play off the Mohammedan against the Hindu population. But now that a pronounced revolutionary and nationalist tendency shows itself among these latter, the danger is imminent that Pan-Islamism, thoroughly roused, should unite with the revolutionary elements of Bengal. The co-operation of these elements might create a very grave danger, capable of shaking the foundations of England's high position in the world. . . .

All these circumstances constitute a grave menace to the stability of England's Empire, and these dangers largely influence England's attitude towards Germany.

England may have to tolerate the rivalry of North America in her imperial and commercial ambitions, but the competition of Germany must be stopped. If England is forced to fight America, the German fleet must not be in a position to help the Americans. Therefore it must be destroyed.

A similar line of thought is suggested by the eventuality of a great English colonial war, which would engage England's fleets in far distant parts of the world. England knows the German needs and capabilities of expansion, and may well fear

9. "Divide and rule."

that a German Empire with a strong fleet might use such an opportunity for obtaining that increase of territory which England grudges. We may thus explain the apparent indifference of England to the French schemes of aggrandizement. France's capability of expansion is exhausted from insufficient increase of population. She can no longer be dangerous to England as a nation, and would soon fall victim to English lust of Empire, if only Germany were conquered.

The wish to get rid of the dangers presumably threatening from the German quarter is all the more real since geographical conditions offer a prospect of crippling the German overseas commerce without any excessive efforts. The comparative weakness of the German fleet, contrasted with the vast superiority of the English navy, allows a correspondingly easy victory to be anticipated, especially if the French fleet co-operates. The possibility, therefore, of quickly and completely getting rid of one rival, in order to have a free hand for all other contingencies, looms very near and undoubtedly presents a practicable means of placing the naval power of England on a firm footing for years to come, of annihilating German commerce and of checking the importance of German interests in Africa and Northern Asia.

The hostility to Germany is also sufficiently evident in other matters. It has always been England's object to maintain a certain balance of power between the continental nations of Europe, and to prevent any one of them attaining a pronounced supremacy. While these States crippled and hindered each other from playing any active part on the world's stage, England acquired an opportunity of following out her own purposes undisturbed, and of founding that world Empire which she now holds. This policy she still continues, for so long as the Powers of Europe tie each other's hands, her own supremacy is uncontested. It follows directly from this that England's aim must be to repress Germany, but strengthen France; for Germany at the present moment is the only European State which threatens to win a commanding position; but France is her born rival, and cannot keep on level terms with her stronger neighbour on the East, unless she adds to her forces and is helped by her allies. Thus the hostility to Germany, from this aspect also, is based on England's most important interests, and we must treat it as axiomatic and self-evident.

The argument is often adduced that England by a war with Germany would chiefly injure herself, since she would lose the German market, which is the best purchaser of her industrial products, and would be deprived of the very considerable German import trade. I fear that from the English point of view these conditions would be an additional incentive to war. England would hope to acquire, in place of the lost German market, a large part of those markets which had been supplied by Germany before the war, and the want of German imports would be a great stimulus, and to some extent a great benefit, to English industries.

After all, it is from the English aspect of the question quite comprehensible that the English Government strains every nerve to check the growing power of Germany, and that a passionate desire prevails in large circles of the English nation to destroy the German fleet which is building, and attack the objectionable neighbour.

English policy might, however, strike out a different line, and attempt to come to terms with Germany instead of fighting. This would be the most desirable course for us. A Triple Alliance— Germany, England, and America—has been suggested.[10] But for such a union with Germany to be possible, England must have resolved to give a free course to German development side by side with her own, to allow the enlargement of our colonial power, and to offer no political hindrances to our commercial and industrial competition. She must, therefore, have renounced her traditional policy, and contemplate an entirely new grouping of the Great Powers in the world.

10. Thomas Schiemann, "The United States and the War Cloud in Europe," *McClure's Magazine*, June 1910.

It cannot be assumed that English pride and self-interest will consent to that. The continuous agitation against Germany, under the tacit approval of the Government, which is kept up not only by the majority of the Press, but by a strong party in the country, the latest statements of English politicians, the military preparations in the North Sea, and the feverish acceleration of naval construction, are unmistakable indications that England intends to persist in her anti-German policy. The uncompromising hostility of England and her efforts to hinder every expansion of Germany's power were openly shown in the very recent Morocco question. Those who think themselves capable of impressing on the world the stamp of their spirit, do not resign the headship without a struggle, when they think victory is in their grasp.

A pacific agreement with England is, after all, a will-o'-the-wisp which no serious German statesman would trouble to follow. We must always keep the possibility of war with England before our eyes, and arrange our political and military plans accordingly. We need not concern ourselves with any pacific protestations of English politicians, publicists, and Utopians, which, prompted by the exigencies of the moment, cannot alter the real basis of affairs. When the Unionists,[11] with their greater fixity of purpose, replace the Liberals at the helm, we must be prepared for a vigorous assertion of power by the island Empire. . . .

While the aspiring Great Powers of the Far East cannot at present directly influence our policy, Turkey—the predominant Power of the Near East—is of paramount importance to us. She is our natural ally; it is emphatically our interest to keep in close touch with her. The wisest course would have been to have made her earlier a member of the Triple Alliance, and so to have prevented the Turco-Italian War, which threatens to change the whole political situation, to our disadvantage. Turkey would gain in two ways: she assures her position both against Russia and against England—the two States, that is, with whose hostility we have to reckon. Turkey, also, is the only Power which can threaten England's position in Egypt, and thus menace the short sea-route and the land communications to India. We ought to spare no sacrifices to secure this country as an ally for the eventuality of a war with England or Russia. Turkey's interests are ours. It is also to the obvious advantage of Italy that Turkey maintain her commanding position on the Bosphorus and at the Dardanelles, that this important key should not be transferred to the keeping of foreigners, and belong to Russia or England.

If Russia gained the access to the Mediterranean, to which she has so long aspired, she would soon become a prominent Power in its eastern basin, and thus greatly damage the Italian projects in those waters. Since the English interests, also, would be prejudiced by such a development, the English fleet in the Mediterranean would certainly be strengthened. Between England, France, and Russia it would be quite impossible for Italy to attain an independent or commanding position, while the opposition of Russia and Turkey leaves the field open to her. From this view of the question, therefore, it is advisable to end the Turco-Italian conflict, and to try and satisfy the justifiable wishes of Italy at the cost of France. . . .

If we look at these conditions as a whole, it appears that on the continent of Europe the power of the Central European Triple Alliance and that of the States united against it by alliance and agreement balance each other, provided that Italy belongs to the league. If we take into calculation the imponderabilia,[12] whose weight can only be guessed at, the scale is inclined slightly in favour of the Triple Alliance. On the other hand, England indisputably rules the sea. In consequence of her crushing naval superiority when allied with

11. That is, the Conservatives and their allies, the Liberal Unionists, who broke with the rest of the Liberal Party over home rule for Ireland.

12. The unknown factors.

France, and of the geographical conditions, she may cause the greatest damage to Germany by cutting off her maritime trade. There is also a not inconsiderable army available for a continental war. When all considerations are taken into account, our opponents have a political superiority not to be underestimated. If France succeeds in strengthening her army by large colonial levies and a strong English landing-force, this superiority would be asserted on land also. If Italy really withdraws from the Triple Alliance, very distinctly superior forces will be united against Germany and Austria.

Under these conditions the position of Germany is extraordinarily difficult. We not only require for the full material development of our nation, on a scale corresponding to its intellectual importance, an extended political basis, but . . . we are compelled to obtain space for our increasing population and markets for our growing industries. But at every step which we take in this direction England will resolutely oppose us. English policy may not yet have made the definite decision to attack us; but it doubtless wishes, by all and every means, even the most extreme, to hinder every further expansion of German international influence and of German maritime power. The recognized political aims of England and the attitude of the English Government leave no doubt on this point. But if we were involved in a struggle with England, we can be quite sure that France would not neglect the opportunity of attacking our flank. Italy, with her extensive coast-line, even if still a member of the Triple Alliance, will have to devote large forces to the defence of the coast to keep off the attacks of the Anglo-French Mediterranean Fleet, and would thus be only able to employ weaker forces against France. Austria would be paralyzed by Russia; against the latter we should have to leave forces in the East. We should thus have to fight out the struggle against France and England practically alone with a part of our army, perhaps with some support from Italy. It is in this double menace by sea and on the mainland of Europe that the grave danger to our political position lies, since all freedom of action is taken from us and all expansion barred.

Since the struggle is, as appears on a thorough investigation of the international question, necessary and inevitable, we must fight it out, cost what it may. Indeed, we are carrying it on at the present moment, though not with drawn swords, and only by peaceful means so far. On the one hand it is being waged by the competition in trade, industries and warlike preparations; on the other hand, by diplomatic methods with which the rival States are fighting each other in every region where their interests clash.

With these methods it has been possible to maintain peace hitherto, but not without considerable loss of power and prestige. This apparently peaceful state of things must not deceive us; we are facing a hidden, but none the less formidable, crisis—perhaps the most momentous crisis in the history of the German nation.

We have fought in the last great wars for our national union and our position among the Powers of Europe; we now must decide whether we wish to develop into and maintain a World Empire, and procure for German spirit and German ideas that fit recognition which has been hitherto withheld from them.

Have we the energy to aspire to that great goal? Are we prepared to make the sacrifices which such an effort will doubtless cost us? or are we willing to recoil before the hostile forces, and sink step by step lower in our economic, political, and national importance? That is what is involved in our decision.

"To be, or not to be," is the question which is put to us to-day, disguised, indeed, by the apparent equilibrium of the opposing interests and forces, by the deceitful shifts of diplomacy, and the official peace-aspirations of all the States; but by the logic of history inexorably demanding an answer, if we look with clear gaze beyond the narrow horizon of the day and the mere surface of things into the region of realities.

There is no standing still in the world's history. All is growth and development. It is obviously impossible to keep things in the *status quo*, as diplomacy has so often attempted. No true statesman will ever seriously count on such a possibility; he will only make the outward and temporary maintenance of existing conditions a duty when he wishes to gain time and deceive an opponent, or when he cannot see what is the trend of events. He will use such diplomatic means only as inferior tools; in reality he will only reckon with actual forces and with the powers of a continuous development.

We must make it quite clear to ourselves that there can be no standing still, no being satisfied for us, but only progress or retrogression, and that it is tantamount to retrogression when we are contented with our present place among the nations of Europe, while all our rivals are straining with desperate energy, even at the cost of our rights, to extend their power. The process of our decay would set in gradually and advance slowly so long as the struggle against us was waged with peaceful weapons; the living generation would, perhaps, be able to continue to exist in peace and comfort. But should a war be forced upon us by stronger enemies under conditions unfavourable to us, then, if our arms met with disaster, our political downfall would not be delayed, and we should rapidly sink down. The future of German nationality would be sacrificed, an independent German civilization would not long exist, and the blessings for which German blood has flowed in streams—spiritual and moral liberty, and the profound and lofty aspirations of German thought—would for long ages be lost to mankind.

If, as is right, we do not wish to assume the responsibility for such a catastrophe, we must have the courage to strive with every means to attain that increase of power which we are entitled to claim, even at the risk of a war with numerically superior foes.

Under present conditions it is out of the question to attempt this by acquiring territory in Europe.

The region in the East, where German colonists once settled, is lost to us, and could only be recovered from Russia by a long and victorious war, and would then be a perpetual incitement to renewed wars. So, again, the reannexation of the former South Prussia, which was united to Prussia on the second partition of Poland, would be a serious undertaking, on account of the Polish population.

Under these circumstances we must clearly try to strengthen our political power in other ways.

In the first place, our political position would be considerably consolidated if we could finally get rid of the standing danger that France will attack us on a favourable occasion, so soon as we find ourselves involved in complications elsewhere. In one way or another *we must square our account with France* if we wish for a free hand in our international policy. This is the first and foremost condition of a sound German policy, and since the hostility of France once for all cannot be removed by peaceful overtures, the matter must be settled by force of arms. France must be so completely crushed that she can never again come across our path.

Further, we must contrive every means of strengthening the political power of our allies. We have already followed such a policy in the case of Austria when we declared our readiness to protect, if necessary with armed intervention, the final annexation of Bosnia and Herzegovina by our ally on the Danube. Our policy towards Italy must follow the same lines, especially if in any Franco-German war an opportunity should be presented of doing her a really valuable service. It is equally good policy in every way to support Turkey, whose importance for Germany and the Triple Alliance has already been discussed.

Our political duties, therefore, are complicated, and during the Turco-Italian War all that we can do at first is to use our influence as mediators, and to prevent a transference of hostilities to the Balkan Peninsula. It cannot be decided at this moment whether further intervention will be necessary. Finally, as regards our own position in

Europe, we can only effect an extension of our own political influence, in my opinion, by awakening in our weaker neighbours, through the integrity and firmness of our policy, the conviction that their independence and their interests are bound up with Germany, and are best secured under the protection of the German arms. This conviction might eventually lead to an enlargement of the Triple Alliance into a Central European Federation. Our military strength in Central Europe would by this means be considerably increased, and the extraordinarily unfavourable geographical configuration of our dominions would be essentially improved in case of war. Such a federation would be the expression of a natural community of interests, which is founded on the geographical and natural conditions, and would insure the durability of the political community based on it.

We must employ other means also for the widening of our colonial territory, so that it may be able to receive the overflow of our population. It is possible to obtain districts in Equatorial Africa by pacific negotiations. . . . . If necessary, they must be obtained as the result of a successful European war. In all these possible acquisitions of territory the point must be strictly borne in mind that we require countries which are climatically suited to German settlers. Now, there are even in Central Africa large regions which are adapted to the settlement of German farmers and stock-breeders, and part of our overflow population might be diverted to those parts. But, generally speaking, we can only obtain in tropical colonies markets for our industrial products and wide stretches of cultivated ground for the growth of the raw materials which our industries require. This represents in itself a considerable advantage, but does not release us from the obligation to acquire land for actual colonization. . . .

The execution of such political schemes would certainly clash with many old-fashioned notions and vested rights of the traditional European policy. In the first place, the principle of the balance of power in Europe, which has, since the Congress of Vienna, led an almost sacrosanct but entirely unjustifiable existence, must be entirely disregarded.

The idea of a balance of power was gradually developed from the feeling that States do not exist to thwart each other, but to work together for the advancement of culture. Christianity, which leads man beyond the limits of the State to a world citizenship of the noblest kind, and lays the foundation of all international law, has exercised a wide influence in this respect. Practical interests, too, have strengthened the theory of balance of power. When it was understood that the State was a power, and that, by its nature, it must strive to extend that power, a certain guarantee of peace was supposed to exist in the balance of forces. The conviction was thus gradually established that every State had a close community of interests with the other States, with which it entered into political and economic relations, and was bound to establish some sort of understanding with them. Thus the idea grew up in Europe of a State-system, which was formed after the fall of Napoleon by the five Great Powers—England, France, Russia, Austria, and Prussia, which latter had gained a place in the first rank by force of arms; in 1866 Italy joined it as the sixth Great Power.

"Such a system cannot be supported with an approximate equilibrium among the nations." "All theory must rest on the basis of practice, and a real equilibrium—an actual equality of power—is postulated."[13] This condition does not exist between the European nations. England by herself rules the sea, and the 65,000,000 of Germans cannot allow themselves to sink to the same level of power as the 40,000,000 of French. An attempt has been made to produce a real equilibrium by special alliances. One result only has been obtained—the hindrance of the free development of the nations in general, and of Germany in particular. This is an unsound condition. A European balance of power can no longer be termed a

13. The quotes are from Treitschke.

condition which corresponds to the existing state of things; it can only have the disastrous consequences of rendering the forces of the continental European States mutually ineffective, and of thus favouring the plans of the political powers which stand outside that charmed circle. It has always been England's policy to stir up enmity between the respective continental States, and to keep them at approximately the same standard of power, in order herself undisturbed to conquer at once the sovereignty of the seas and the sovereignty of the world.

We must put aside all such notions of equilibrium. In its present distorted form it is opposed to our weightiest interests. The idea of a State system which has common interests in civilization must not, of course, be abandoned; but it must be expanded on a new and more just basis. It is now not a question of a European State system, but of one embracing all the States in the world, in which the equilibrium is established on real factors of power. We must endeavour to obtain in this system our merited position at the head of a federation of Central European States, and thus reduce the imaginary European equilibrium, in one way or the other, to its true value, and correspondingly to increase our own power.

A further question, suggested by the present political position, is whether all the political treaties which were concluded at the beginning of the last century under quite other conditions—in fact, under a different conception of what constitutes a State—can, or ought to be, permanently observed. When Belgium was proclaimed neutral, no one contemplated that she would lay claim to a large and valuable region of Africa. It may well be asked whether the acquisition of such territory is not *ipso facto* a breach of neutrality, for a State from which—theoretically at least—all danger of war has been removed, has no right to enter into political competition with the other States. This argument is the more justifiable because it may safely be assumed that, in event of a war of

Germany against France and England, the two last mentioned States would try to unite their forces in Belgium. Lastly, the neutrality of the Congo State[14] must be termed more than problematic, since Belgium claims the right to cede or sell it to a non-neutral country. The conception of permanent neutrality is entirely contrary to the essential nature of the State, which can only attain its highest moral aims in competition with other States. Its complete development presupposes such competition.

Again, the principle that no State can ever interfere in the internal affairs of another State is repugnant to the highest rights of the State. This principle is, of course, very variously interpreted, and powerful States have never refrained from a higher-handed interference in the internal affairs of smaller ones. We daily witness instances of such conduct. Indeed, England quite lately attempted to interfere in the private affairs of Germany, not formally or by diplomatic methods, but none the less in point of fact, on the subject of our naval preparations. It is, however, accepted as a principle of international intercourse that between the States of one and the same political system a strict non-interference in home affairs should be observed. The unqualified recognition of this principle and its application to political intercourse under all conditions involves serious difficulties. It is the doctrine of the Liberals, which was first preached in France in 1830, and of which the English Ministry of Lord Palmerston availed themselves for their own purpose. Equally false is the doctrine of unrestricted intervention, as promulgated by the States of the Holy Alliance at Troppau in 1820. No fixed principles for international politics can be laid down.

After all, the relation of States to each other is that of individuals; and as the individual can decline the interference of others in his affairs, so

14. The Congo State was proclaimed neutral, but without guarantees, by Acts of February 26, 1885.

naturally, the same right belongs to the State. Above the individual, however, stands the authority of the State, which regulates the relations of the citizens to each other. But no one stands above the State; it is sovereign and must itself decide whether the internal conditions or measures of another state menace its own existence or interests. In no case, therefore, may a sovereign State renounce the right of interfering in the affairs of other States, should circumstances demand. Cases may occur at any time, when the party disputes or the preparations of the neighboring country becomes a threat to the existence of a State. "It can only be asserted that every State acts at its own risk when it interferes in the internal affairs of another State, and that experience shows how very dangerous such an interference may become." On the other hand, it must be remembered that the dangers which may arise from non-intervention are occasionally still graver, and that the whole discussion turns, not on an international right, but simply and solely on power and expediency.

I have gone closely into these questions of international policy because, under conditions which are not remote, they may greatly influence the realization of our necessary political aspirations, and may give rise to hostile complications. Then it becomes essential that we do not allow ourselves to be cramped in our freedom of action by considerations, devoid of any inherent political necessity, which only depend on political expediency, and are not binding on us. We must remain conscious in all such eventualities that we cannot, under any circumstances, avoid fighting for our position in the world, and that the all-important point is, not to postpone that war as long as possible, but to bring it on under the most favourable conditions possible. "No man," so wrote Frederick the Great to Pitt on July 3, 1761, "if he has a grain of sense, will leave his enemies leisure to make all preparations in order to destroy him; he will rather take advantage of his start to put himself in a favourable position. . . ."

Source: Friedrich von Bernhardi, Germany and the Next War, *http://www.fullbooks.com/Germany-and-the-Next-War1.html, accessed November 19, 2019.*

THE ULSTER COVENANT AND DECLARATION (1912)

As it became increasingly likely that Parliament would pass home rule for Ireland, the following was circulated in Northern Ireland in September 1912. Nearly 250,000 men signed the Covenant, while a similar number of women signed the Declaration. In early 1913 the Ulster Volunteers, a militia unit formed to fight against home rule, recruited some 100,000 men from among the signers of the Covenant.

The Covenant (for men)

Being convinced in our consciences that Home Rule would be disastrous to the material well-being of Ulster as well as of the whole of Ireland, subversive of our civil and religious freedom, destructive of our citizenship and perilous to the unity of the Empire, we, whose names are underwritten, men of Ulster, loyal subjects of his Gracious Majesty King George V, humbly relying on the God whom our fathers in days of stress and trial confidently trusted, do hereby pledge ourselves in solemn Covenant throughout this our time of threatened calamity to stand by one another in defending for ourselves and our children our cherished position of equal citizenship in the United Kingdom and in using all means which may be found necessary to defeat the present conspiracy to set up a Home Rule Parliament in Ireland. And in the event of such a Parliament being forced upon us we further solemnly and mutually pledge ourselves to refuse to recognise its authority. In sure confidence that God will defend the right we hereto subscribe our names. And further, we individually declare that we have not already signed this Covenant.

The Declaration (for women)

We, whose names are underwritten, women of Ulster, and loyal subjects of our gracious King, being firmly persuaded that Home Rule would be disastrous to our Country, desire to associate ourselves with the men of Ulster in their uncompromising opposition to the Home Rule Bill now before Parliament, whereby it is proposed to drive Ulster out of her cherished place in the Constitution of the United Kingdom, and to place her under the domination and control of a Parliament in Ireland.

Praying that from this calamity God will save Ireland, we here to subscribe our names.

Ulster Day, Saturday 28th, September, 1912.

God Save the King

Source: The 1912 Ulster Covenant, History Ireland, https://www.historyireland.com/20th-century -contemporary-history/the-1912-ulster-covenant-by -joseph-e-a-connell-jr/, accessed November 19, 2019.

FIFTH TREATY OF THE TRIPLE ALLIANCE (1912)

Originally concluded in 1882, the Triple Alliance was renewed four times before 1914. The treaty lay at the heart of Bismarck's strategy to keep France isolated. The Dual Alliance between Germany and Austria-Hungary dated back to 1879; Italy, embroiled in a dispute with France over North Africa, adhered to the agreement three years later. In the early twentieth century, growing tensions between Austria-Hungary and Italy raised questions of whether Rome would actually go to war on Vienna's behalf. Nevertheless, the three powers reaffirmed the agreement in December 1912. Members of the German, Austro-Hungarian, and Italian factions should be familiar with the terms of this treaty and know what their responsibilities are in the event of war.

Treaty of Alliance between Austria-Hungary, the German Empire, and Italy. Vienna, December 5, 1912.

Their Majesties the Emperor of Austria, King of Bohemia, etc., and Apostolic King of Hungary, the Emperor of Germany, King of Prussia, and the King of Italy, firmly resolved to assure to Their States the continuation of the benefits which the maintenance of the Triple Alliance guarantees to them, from the political point of view as well as from the monarchical and social point of view, and wishing with this object to prolong the duration of this Alliance, concluded on May 20, 1882, renewed a first time by the Treaties of February 20, 1887, a second time by the Treaty of May 6, 1891, and a third time by the Treaty of June 28, 1902, have, for this purpose, appointed as Their Plenipotentiaries, to wit:

His Majesty the Emperor of Austria, King of Bohemia, etc., and Apostolic King of Hungary: Count Leopold Berchtold von und zu Ungarschitz, His Minister of the Imperial and Royal Household and of Foreign Affairs, President of the Common Council of Ministers; His Majesty the Emperor of Germany, King of Prussia: the Sieur Heinrich von Tschirschky und Bogendorff, His Ambassador Extraordinary and Plenipotentiary to His Majesty the Emperor of Austria, King of Bohemia, etc., and Apostolic King of Hungary; and His Majesty the King of Italy: Duke Giuseppe d'Avarna, His Ambassador Extraordinary and Plenipotentiary to His Majesty the Emperor of Austria, King of Bohemia, etc., and Apostolic King of Hungary, who, after exchange of their full powers, found in good and due form, have agreed upon the following Articles:

ARTICLE 1

The High Contracting Parties mutually promise peace and friendship, and will enter into no alliance or engagement directed against any one of their States.

They engage to proceed to an exchange of ideas on political and economic questions of a general nature which may arise, and they further promise one another mutual support within the limits of their own interests.

ARTICLE 2

In case Italy, without direct provocation on her part, should be attacked by France for any reason whatsoever, the two other Contracting Parties shall be bound to lend help and assistance with all their forces to the Party attacked.

This same obligation shall devolve upon Italy in case of any aggression without direct provocation by France against Germany.

Article 3

If one, or two, of the High Contracting Parties, without direct provocation on their part, should chance to be attacked and to be engaged in a war with two or more Great Powers nonsignatory to the present Treaty, the casus foederis will arise simultaneously for all the High Contracting Parties.

Article 4

In case a Great Power nonsignatory to the present Treaty should threaten the security of the states of one of the High Contracting Parties, and the threatened Party should find itself forced on that account to make war against it, the two others bind themselves to observe towards their Ally a benevolent neutrality. Each of them reserves to itself, in this case, the right to take part in the war, if it should see fit, to make common cause with its Ally.

Article 5

If the peace of one of the High Contracting Parties should chance to be threatened under the circumstances foreseen by the preceding Articles, the High Contracting Parties shall take counsel together in ample time as to the military measures to be taken with a view to eventual cooperation.

They engage, henceforth, in all cases of common participation in a war, to conclude neither armistice, nor peace, nor treaty, except by common agreement among themselves.

Article 6

Germany and Italy, having in mind only the maintenance, so far as possible, of the territorial status quo in the Orient, engage to use their influence to forestall on the Ottoman coasts and islands in the Adriatic and the Aegean Seas any territorial modification which might be injurious to one or the other of the Powers signatory to the present Treaty. To this end, they will communicate

to one another all information of a nature to enlighten each other mutually concerning their own dispositions, as well as those of other Powers.

Article 7

Austria-Hungary and Italy, having in mind only the maintenance, so far as possible, of the territorial status quo in the Orient, engage to use their influence to forestall any territorial modification which might be injurious to one or the other of the Powers signatory to the present Treaty. To this end, they shall communicate to one another all information of a nature to enlighten each other mutually concerning their own dispositions, as well as those of other Powers. However, if, in the course of events, the maintenance of the status quo in the regions of the Balkans or of the Ottoman coasts and islands in the Adriatic and in the Aegean Sea should become impossible, and if, whether in consequence of the action of a third Power or otherwise, Austria-Hungary or Italy should find themselves under the necessity of modifying it by a temporary or permanent occupation on their part, this occupation shall take place only after a previous agreement between the two Powers, based upon the principle of a reciprocal compensation for every advantage, territorial or other, which each of them might obtain beyond the present status quo, and giving satisfaction to the interests and well founded claims of the two Parties.

Article 8

The stipulations of Articles 6 and 7 shall apply in no way to the Egyptian question, with regard to which the High Contracting Parties preserve respectively their freedom of action, regard being always paid to the principles upon which the present Treaty rests.

Article 9

Germany and Italy engage to exert themselves for the maintenance of the territorial status quo in the North African regions on the Mediterranean, to wit, Cyrenaica, Tripolitania, and Tunisia. The Representatives of the two Powers in these regions shall be instructed to put themselves into the closest intimacy of mutual communication and assistance.

If unfortunately, as a result of a mature examination of the situation, Germany and Italy should both recognize that the maintenance of the status quo has become impossible, Germany engages, after a formal and previous agreement, to support Italy in any action in the form of occupation or other taking of guaranty which the latter should undertake in these same regions with a view to an interest of equilibrium and of legitimate compensation.

It is understood that in such an eventuality the two Powers would seek to place themselves likewise in agreement with England.

ARTICLE 10

If it were to happen that France should make a move to extend her occupation, or even her protectorate or her sovereignty, under any form whatsoever, in the North African territories, and that in consequence thereof Italy, in order to safeguard her position in the Mediterranean, should feel that she must herself undertake action in the said North African territories, or even have recourse to extreme measures in French territory in Europe, the state of war which would thereby ensue between Italy and France would constitute ipso facto, on the demand of Italy, and at the common charge of Germany and Italy, the casus foederis foreseen by Articles 2 and 5 of the present Treaty, as if such an eventuality were expressly contemplated therein.

ARTICLE 11

If the fortunes of any war undertaken in common against France by the two Powers should lead Italy to seek for territorial guaranties with respect to France for the security of the frontiers of the Kingdom and of her maritime position, as well as with a view to stability and to peace, Germany will present no obstacle thereto, and, if need be, and in a measure compatible with circumstances, will apply herself to facilitating the means of attaining such a purpose.

ARTICLE 12

The High Contracting Parties mutually promise secrecy as to the contents of the present Treaty.

ARTICLE 13

The Signatory Powers reserve the right of subsequently introducing, in the form of a Protocol and of a common agreement, the modifications of which the utility should be demonstrated by circumstances.

ARTICLE 14

The present Treaty shall remain in force for the space of six years, dating from the expiration of the Treaty now in force; but if it has not been denounced one year in advance by one or another of the High Contracting Parties, it shall remain in force for the same duration of six more years.

ARTICLE 15

The ratifications of the present Treaty shall be exchanged at Vienna within a period of a fortnight, or sooner if may be.

In witness whereof the respective Plenipotentiaries have signed the present Treaty and have affixed thereto the seal of their arms.

Done at Vienna, in triplicate, the fifth day of the month of December, one thousand nine hundred and twelve.

L. S. Berchtold
[Foreign Minister of Austria-Hungary].

L. S. von Tschirschky
[German Ambassador to Austria-Hungary].

L. S. Avarna
[Italian Ambassador to Austria-Hungary].

Source: Alfred Francis Pribram, The Secret Treaties of Austria-Hungary, 1879–1914, Volume 1 *(Cambridge, MA: Harvard University Press, 1920), 245–59.*

TREATY OF ALLIANCE BETWEEN THE KINGDOM OF GREECE AND THE KINGDOM OF SERBIA (1913)

The First Balkan War, which pitted Serbia, Greece, and Bulgaria against the Ottoman Empire, resulted in quick defeat for Turkish forces, but serious disputes arose over how the spoils would be divided. The Bulgarian government claimed the lion's share, arguing that its troops had done the bulk of the fighting. Greece and Serbia rejected this claim, and concluded this alliance.

Signed, May 19/ June 1, 1913; ratifications exchanged at Athens, June 8/21, 1913.

His Majesty the King of the Hellenes and His Majesty the King of Serbia, considering that it is their duty to look after the security of their people and the tranquillity of their kingdoms; considering furthermore, in their firm desire to preserve a durable peace in the Balkan Peninsula, that the most effective means to attain it is to be united by a close defensive alliance;

Have resolved to conclude an alliance of peace, of friendship, and of mutual protection, promising to each other never to give to their purely defensive agreement an offensive character, and for that purpose they have appointed as their plenipotentiaries:

His Majesty the King of the Hellenes; Mr. John Alexandropoulos, his Minister at Belgrade, Commander of the Royal Order of the Savior, Grand Commander of the Royal Order of Takovo; His Majesty the King of Serbia; Mr. Mathias Boschkovitch, his Minister at Athens, Grand Commander of the Royal Order of Saint Sava, Commander of the Royal Order of the Savior, who, after having exchanged their full powers found in good and due form, have today agreed as follows:

ARTICLE 1

The two high contracting parties covenant expressly the mutual guarantee of their possessions and bind themselves, in case, contrary to their hopes, one of the two kingdoms should be attacked without any provocation on its part, to afford to each other assistance with all their armed forces and not to conclude peace subsequently except jointly and together.

ARTICLE 2

At the division of the territories of European Turkey, which will be ceded to the Balkan States after the termination of the present war by the treaty of peace with the Ottoman Empire, the two high contracting parties bind themselves not to come to any separate understanding with Bulgaria, to afford each other constant assistance, and to proceed always together, upholding mutually their territorial claims and the boundary lines hereafter to be indicated.

ARTICLE 3

The two high contracting parties, considering that it is to the vital interest of their kingdoms that no other state should interpose between their respective possessions to the west of the Axios (Vardar) river, declare that they will mutually assist one another in order that Greece and Serbia may have a common boundary line. This boundary line, based on the principle of effective occupation, shall start from the highest summit of the mountain range of Kamna, delimiting the basin of the Upper Schkoumbi, it shall pass round the lake Achris (Ochrida), shall reach the western shore of the Prespa lake in the Kousko village and the eastern shore to the Lower Dupliani (Dolni Dupliani), shall run near Rahmanli, shall follow the line of separation of the waters between the Erigon (Tserna) river and Moglenica and shall reach the Axios (Vardar) river at a distance of nearly three kilometers to the south of Ghevgheh, according to the line drawn in detail in Annex I of the present treaty.

ARTICLE 4

The two high contracting parties agree that the Greco-Bulgarian and Serbo-Bulgarian boundary lines shall be established on the principle of actual possession and the equilibrium between the three states, as follows:

The eastern frontier of Serbia from Ghevgheli shall follow the course of the Axios (Vardar) river up to the confluence of Bojimia-Dere, shall ascend that river, and, passing by the altitudes 120, 350, 754, 895, 571, and the rivers Kriva, Lakavitza, Bregalnica and Zletovska shall proceed towards a point of the old Turkish-Bulgarian frontier on the Osogovska Planina, altitude 2225, according to the line drawn in detail in the Annex II of the present treaty.

The Greek frontier on the side of Bulgaria shall leave to Greece on the left shore of Axios (Vardar) the territories occupied by the Greek and Serbian troops opposite Ghevgheli and Davidovo as far as the mountain Beles and the Doiran lake; then, passing to the south of Kilkitch it shall run through the Strymon river by the north of the Orliako bridge and shall proceed through the Achinos (Tachinos) lake and the Angitis (Anghista) river to the sea, a little to the east of the Gulf of Eleutherai according to the line drawn in detail in the Annex III of the present treaty.

ARTICLE 5

Should a dissension arise with Bulgaria in regard to the frontiers as indicated above, and if every friendly settlement becomes impossible, the two high contracting parties reserve to themselves the right to propose by common agreement, to Bulgaria, that the dispute be submitted to the mediation or arbitration of the sovereigns of the Entente Powers or the chiefs of other states. In case Bulgaria shall refuse to accept this manner of peaceful settlement and assume a menacing attitude against either of the two kingdoms, or attempt to impose her claims by force, the two high contracting parties bind themselves solemnly to afford assistance to each other with all their armed forces and not to conclude peace subsequently except jointly and together.

ARTICLE 6

In order to prepare and to secure the means of military defense, a military convention shall be concluded with the least possible delay from the signature of the present treaty.

ARTICLE 7

His Majesty the King of the Hellenes covenants that his government shall grant all the necessary facilities and guarantees for a period of fifty years for the complete freedom of the export and import trade of Serbia through the port of Salonika and the railway lines from Salonika to Uskup and Monastir. This freedom shall be as large as possible, provided only it is compatible with the full and entire exercise of the Hellenic sovereignty.

A special convention shall be concluded between the two high contracting parties within one year from this day in order to regulate in detail the carrying out of this article.

ARTICLE 8

The two high contracting parties agree that upon the final settlement of all the questions resulting from the present war, the General Staffs of the two armies shall come to an understanding with the view of regulating in a parallel manner the increase of the military forces of each state.

ARTICLE 9

The two high contracting parties agree furthermore that, upon the final settlement of all the questions resulting from the present war, they will proceed by common agreement to the study of a plan of a custom convention, in order to draw closer the commercial and economic relations of the two countries.

ARTICLE 10

The present treaty shall be put in force after its signature. It can not be denounced before the expiration of ten years. The intention for the cessation of its force shall be notified by one of the two high contracting parties to the other six months in advance, in the absence of which the agreement shall continue to be binding upon the two states until the expiration of one year from the date of the denunciation.

ARTICLE 11

The present treaty shall be kept strictly secret. It can not be communicated to another Power either totally or partially, except with the consent of the two high contracting parties.

It shall be ratified as soon as possible. The ratifications shall be exchanged in Athens.

In faith whereof the respective plenipotentiaries have signed this treaty and affixed their seals.

Executed in Salonika, in duplicate, the nineteenth day of May in the year one thousand nine hundred and thirteen.

John Alexandropoulos [Greek Minister to Serbia].

M. Boschkovitch [Serbian Minister to Greece].

Source: "Diplomatic Documents, 1913–1917, Issued by the Greek Government Concerning the Greco-Serbian Treaty of Alliance and the Germano-Bulgarian Invasion in Macedonia: Part First," American Journal of International Law, *12:2 (April 1918), 89–92.*

THE ASSASSINATION OF ARCHDUKE FRANZ FERDINAND, AS RECOUNTED BY HIS BODYGUARD (1914)

Franz Ferdinand and his wife, Sophie, were killed by Serb nationalist Gavrilo Princip while on a formal visit to Sarajevo. Princip shot Ferdinand at point blank range while the latter was traveling in his car from a town hall reception, having earlier that day already survived one assassination attempt. Standing on the car's sideboard was Ferdinand's bodyguard, Count Franz von Harrach. A witness to Ferdinand's assassination, he subsequently recounted the events of the day. A portion of his translated memoir is reproduced below.

As the car quickly reversed, a thin stream of blood spurted from His Highness's mouth onto my right check. As I was pulling out my handkerchief to wipe the blood away from his mouth, the Duchess cried out to him, "For God's sake! What has happened to you?"

At that she slid off the seat and lay on the floor of the car, with her face between his knees.

I had no idea that she too was hit and thought she had simply fainted with fright. Then I heard His Imperial Highness say, "Sophie, Sophie, don't die. Stay alive for the children!"

At that, I seized the Archduke by the collar of his uniform, to stop his head dropping forward and asked him if he was in great pain. He answered me quite distinctly, "It is nothing!"

His face began to twist somewhat but he went on repeating, six or seven times, ever more faintly as he gradually lost consciousness, "It's nothing!"

Then came a brief pause followed by a convulsive rattle in his throat, caused by a loss of blood. This ceased on arrival at the governor's residence.

The two unconscious bodies were carried into the building where their death was soon established.

Source: Assassination of Archduke Ferdinand, 1914, Eyewitness to History, http://www .eyewitnesstohistory.com/duke.htm, accessed November 19, 2019.

EXCERPT FROM KARL MARX AND FRIEDRICH ENGELS, *THE COMMUNIST MANIFESTO* (1848)

The Communist Manifesto *presented the basic outline of Marxist ideology. It traces the historical development of capitalism, which concentrated wealth and power in the hands of the bourgeoisie (who owned the "means of production"—that is, the factories) and inflicted misery on the proletariat, who were forced to sell their labor (for they owned nothing else) in order to survive. Marx and Engels predicted that the bourgeoisie would continue to shrink in number as more and more would be pushed into the proletariat. Eventually the proletarians would become so numerous and miserable that they would rise up to overthrow capitalism. Under the new "dictatorship of the prole-*

tariat" all private property would be abolished, and the oppressive class system would be destroyed once and for all.

The manifesto paid very little attention to international affairs, but the following passage provided the touchstone for most Marxist thinking on the subject. It was also commonly cited by opponents of Marxism as evidence of the movement's dangerous radicalism.

The Communists are further reproached with desiring to abolish countries and nationality.

The working men have no country. We cannot take from them what they have not got. Since the proletariat must first of all acquire political supremacy, must rise to be the leading class of the nation, must constitute itself the nation, it is, so far, itself national, though not in the bourgeois sense of the word.

National differences and antagonisms between peoples are daily more and more vanishing, owing to the development of the bourgeoisie, to freedom of commerce, to the world-market, to uniformity in the mode of production and in the conditions of life corresponding thereto.

The supremacy of the proletariat will cause them to vanish still faster. United action, of the leading civilized countries at least, is one of the first conditions for the emancipation of the proletariat.

In proportion as the exploitation of one individual by another is put an end to, the exploitation of one nation by another will also be put an end to. In proportion as the antagonism between classes within the nation vanishes, the hostility of one nation to another will come to an end.

Source: Karl Marx and Friedrich Engels, Manifesto of the Communist Party: II. Proletarians and Communists, The Avalon Project, https://avalon.law .yale.edu/19th_century/mantwo.asp, accessed November 19, 2019.

ERFURT PROGRAM (1891)

At a mass party meeting at Erfurt in 1891, the German Social Democratic Party endorsed the following program. Note that while it continues to call for Marxist revolution, it also provides evidence of a new practical orientation within the party—one that encouraged its members to work through existing political institutions. The resignation of Bismarck a year earlier and the expiration of the ban on socialist organizations had ended a state-sanctioned policy of persecution against the party.

In the elections of 1912, the Social Democratic Party received more votes than any other political party, and therefore had a plurality (although far from a majority) of seats in the Reichstag in 1914.

The economic development of bourgeois society invariably leads to the ruin of small business, which is based on the private ownership by the worker of his means of production. It separates the worker from his means of production and turns him into a propertyless proletarian, while the means of production become the monopoly of a relatively small number of capitalists and large landowners.

Hand in hand with this monopolization of the means of production goes the displacement of these fractured small businesses by colossal large enterprises, the development of the tool into a machine, the gigantic growth in the productivity of human labor. But all the benefits of this transformation are monopolized by the capitalists and large landowners. For the proletariat and the sinking middle classes—petty bourgeoisie and farmers—it means an increase in the insecurity of their existence, of misery, of pressure, of oppression, of degradation, of exploitation.

Ever greater becomes the number of proletarians, ever more massive the army of excess workers, ever more stark the opposition between exploiters and the exploited, ever more bitter the class struggle between the bourgeoisie and the proletariat, which divides modern society into two hostile camps and constitutes the common characteristic of all industrialized countries.

The gulf between the propertied and the propertyless is further widened by crises that are grounded in the nature of the capitalist mode of production, crises that are becoming more extensive and more devastating, that elevate this general uncertainty into the normal state of society and furnish proof that the powers of productivity have grown beyond society's control, that the private ownership of the means of production has become incompatible with their appropriate application and full development.

The private ownership of the means of production, once the means for securing for the producer the ownership of his product, has today become the means for expropriating farmers, artisans, and small merchants, and for putting the non-workers—capitalists, large landowners—into possession of the product of the workers. Only the transformation of the capitalist private ownership of the means of production—land and soil, pits and mines, raw materials, tools, machines, means of transportation—into social property and the transformation of the production of goods into socialist production carried on by and for society can cause the large enterprise and the constantly growing productivity of social labor to change for the hitherto exploited classes from a source of misery and oppression into a source of the greatest welfare and universal, harmonious perfection.

This social transformation amounts to the emancipation not only of the proletariat, but of the entire human race, which is suffering from current conditions. But it can only be the work of the working class, because all other classes, notwithstanding the conflicts of interest between them, stand on the ground of the private ownership of the means of production and have as their common goal the preservation of the foundations of contemporary society.

The struggle of the working class against capitalist exploitation is necessarily a political struggle. Without political rights, the working class cannot carry on its economic struggles and develop its economic organization. It cannot bring about the transfer of the means of production into the possession of the community without first having obtained political power.

It is the task of the Social Democratic Party to shape the struggle of the working class into a conscious and unified one and to point out the inherent necessity of its goals.

The interests of the working class are the same in all countries with a capitalist mode of production. With the expansion of global commerce, and of production for the world market, the position of the worker in every country becomes increasingly dependent on the position of workers in other countries. The emancipation of the working class is thus a task in which the workers of all civilized countries are equally involved. Recognizing this, the German Social Democratic Party feels and declares itself to be one with the class-conscious workers of all other countries.

The German Social Democratic Party therefore does not fight for new class privileges and class rights, but for the abolition of class rule and of classes themselves, for equal rights and equal obligations for all, without distinction of sex or birth. Starting from these views, it fights not only the exploitation and oppression of wage earners in society today, but every manner of exploitation and oppression, whether directed against a class, party, sex, or race.

Proceeding from these principles, the German Social Democratic Party demands, first of all:

1. Universal, equal, and direct suffrage with secret ballot in all elections, for all citizens of the Reich over the age of twenty, without distinction of sex. Proportional representation, and, until this is introduced, legal redistribution of electoral districts after every census. Two-year legislative periods. Holding of elections on a legal holiday. Compensation for elected representatives. Suspension of every restriction on political rights, except in the case of legal incapacity.
2. Direct legislation by the people through the rights of proposal and rejection. Self-

determination and self-government of the people in Reich, state, province, and municipality. Election by the people of magistrates, who are answerable and liable to them. Annual voting of taxes.

3. Education of all to bear arms. Militia in the place of the standing army. Determination by the popular assembly on questions of war and peace. Settlement of all international disputes by arbitration.

4. Abolition of all laws that place women at a disadvantage compared with men in matters of public or private law.

5. Abolition of all laws that limit or suppress the free expression of opinion and restrict or suppress the right of association and assembly. Declaration that religion is a private matter. Abolition of all expenditures from public funds for ecclesiastical and religious purposes. Ecclesiastical and religious communities are to be regarded as private associations that regulate their affairs entirely autonomously.

6. Secularization of schools. Compulsory attendance at the public *Volksschule* [extended elementary school]. Free education, free educational materials, and free meals in the public *Volksschulen*, as well as at higher educational institutions for those boys and girls considered qualified for further education by virtue of their abilities.

7. Free administration of justice and free legal assistance. Administration of the law by judges elected by the people. Appeal in criminal cases. Compensation for individuals unjustly accused, imprisoned, or sentenced. Abolition of capital punishment.

8. Free medical care, including midwifery and medicines. Free burial.

9. Graduated income and property tax for defraying all public expenditures, to the extent that they are to be paid for by taxation. Inheritance tax, graduated according to the size of the inheritance and the degree of kinship. Abolition of all indirect taxes, customs, and other economic measures that sacrifice the interests of the community to those of a privileged few.

For the protection of the working classes, the German Social Democratic Party demands, first of all:

1. Effective national and international worker protection laws on the following principles:
   (a) Fixing of a normal working day not to exceed eight hours.
   (b) Prohibition of gainful employment for children under the age of fourteen.
   (c) Prohibition of night work, except in those industries that require night work for inherent technical reasons or for reasons of public welfare.
   (d) An uninterrupted rest period of at least thirty-six hours every week for every worker.
   (e) Prohibition of the truck system.

2. Supervision of all industrial establishments, investigation and regulation of working conditions in the cities and the countryside by a Reich labor department, district labor bureaus, and chambers of labor. Rigorous industrial hygiene.

3. Legal equality of agricultural laborers and domestic servants with industrial workers; abolition of the laws governing domestics.

4. Safeguarding of the freedom of association.

5. Takeover by the Reich government of the entire system of workers' insurance, with decisive participation by the workers in its administration.

Source: The Erfurt Program (1891), *German History in Documents and Images, http://www .germanhistorydocs.ghi-dc.org/sub_document.cfm ?document_id=766.*

The final decades of the nineteenth century in France saw the rise of a number of radical organizations dedicated to Marxian socialism. The most significant difference among them involved their willingness to participate in the politics of the French Republic. The French Socialist Party, founded in 1902 by Jean Jaurés, believed that socialists could achieve at least some of their objectives through participation in "bourgeois" governments. The Socialist Party of France, on the other hand, preferred to stay aloof from politics and instead focus on revolutionary agitation. Under pressure from the Second International, the various parties merged in 1905 to form the French Section of the Workers' International (SFIO), committed to the following program.

The delegates of the French organizations—the Revolutionary Socialist Workers' Party, the Socialist Party of France, the French Socialist Party, the Independent Federations, etc.—declare that the action of the Unified Socialist Party must be based on the principles which have been established by the international congresses, especially the most recent ones at Paris in 1900 and at Amsterdam in 1904.

They state that the divergences of views and different interpretations of tactics, which have so far been able to appear, are due above all to circumstances peculiar to France and to the absence of a general organization.

They affirm their common desire to found a party of the class war which, even while it takes advantage for the workers of minor conflicts among the rich, or is by chance able to concert its action with that of a political party for the defense of the rights or interests of the proletariat, remains always a party of fundamental and unyielding opposition to the whole of the bourgeois class and to the State which is its instrument.

Consequently, the delegates declare that their organizations are ready to collaborate forthwith in this work of unifying the socialist forces on the following bases:

1. The Socialist Party is a class party whose aim is to socialize the means of production and distribution, that is to transform capitalist society into a collectivist or communist society, and to adopt as its means the economic or political organization of the proletariat. By its purpose, its ideal, by the means it adopts, the Socialist Party, while pursuing the achievement of the immediate reforms claimed by the working class, is not a party of reform but a party of class war and revolution.

2. Those whom it returns to Parliament form a single group as compared with all the bourgeois political sects. The Socialist group in Parliament must refuse the Government all the resources which ensure the power of the bourgeoisie and its domination, must refuse, therefore, military credits, credits for colonial conquests, secret funds and the whole of the budget. Even in exceptional circumstances, those returned cannot commit the Party without its consent. In Parliament the Socialist group must dedicate itself to the defense and the extension of the political liberties and rights of the workers, to the pursuit and realization of reforms such as will improve the conditions of life and advance the struggle of the working class. Deputies, like all other selected members, must hold themselves at the disposition of the Party, to serve its action in the country, its general propaganda for organizing the proletariat, and the final ends of socialism.

Articles 3 to 7 assert the authority of the party over all its elected representatives and over the party press, exacting from deputies a portion of their parliamentary salaries and obedience to a mandat impératif—*that is, to prior instructions given to deputies by the party organization. The statement also proposes a Congress of Unity to be held as soon as possible.*

Source: David Thomson, ed., France: Empire and Republic, 1850–1940 *(New York: Harper & Row, 1968), 283–84.*

EXCERPTS FROM A RESOLUTION OF THE INTERNATIONAL SOCIALIST CONGRESS AT STUTTGART (1907)

Nearly 900 delegates from around the world attended the International Socialist Congress held at Stuttgart in August 1907. The delegates passed resolutions on women's rights, colonialism, and immigration, but the main item on the agenda was militarism. There were increasing fears that a European war was imminent, and the congress sought to clarify the appropriate position for socialists around the world to adopt toward foreign affairs. Among those who approved the following resolution were leading figures of the German Social Democratic Party and the French SFIO. Players who seek to establish that socialists are likely to sabotage their countries' war efforts may look to this document for support.

Wars between capitalist states, generally, result from their competitive struggle for world markets, for each state strives not only to assure for itself the markets it already possesses, but also to conquer new ones; in this the subjugation of foreign peoples and countries comes to play a leading role. Furthermore, these wars are caused by the incessant competition in armaments that characterizes militarism, the chief instrument of bourgeois class rule and of the economic and political subjugation of the working class.

Wars are promoted by national prejudices which are systematically cultivated among civilized peoples in the interest of the ruling classes for the purpose of diverting the proletarian masses from their own class problems as well as from their duties of international class solidarity.

Hence, wars are part of the very nature of capitalism; they will cease only when the capitalist economic order is abolished or when the number of sacrifices in men and money, required by the advance in military technique, and the indignation provoked by armaments drive the peoples to abolish this order.

For this reason, the working class, which provides most of the soldiers and makes most of the material sacrifices, is a natural opponent of war, for war contradicts its aim—the creation of an economic order on a socialist basis for the purpose of bringing about the solidarity of all peoples. . . .

If a war threatens to break out, it is the duty of the working class and of its parliamentary representatives in the countries involved, supported by the consolidating activity of the International [Socialist] Bureau, to exert every effort to prevent the outbreak of war by means they consider most effective, which naturally vary according to the accentuation of the class struggle and of the general political situation.

Should war break out none the less, it is their duty to intervene in favor of its speedy termination and to do all in their power to utilize the economic and political crisis caused by the war to rouse the peoples and thereby to hasten the abolition of capitalist class rule.

Source: Olga Hess Gankin and H. H. Fisher, eds., The Bolsheviks and the World War: The Origin of the Third International *(Stanford, CA: Stanford University Press, 1940), 57–59.*

"TO REPUBLICANS" (1913)

This editorial appeared in Le Bonnet Rouge, *an anarchist newspaper published in Paris. Although it did not use Marxist rhetoric—appealing to "Republicans" as opposed to members of the working class—it certainly heightened the fears of nationalists that there might be public unrest in the event of a war against Germany.*

To Republicans:

A poisoned atmosphere hangs over the country. The French people have lost confidence even in themselves. Reaction again takes the offensive and the Republic knows anew the attack of the Calottes.[15]

The reason?

The powerlessness of the Republic to make good its promises.

The Republic has an excuse: if it has not realized all the hopes that the people have placed in it and met all its engagements, it is because since its birth a terrible evil has depressed the world: the folly of armaments. Caught in the whirlwind, France has had to follow, and it can be said that the Republican regime has certainly prevented us going further into madness, but the hour has come to put an end to it.

All, or nearly all, of the national wealth falls into the bottomless pit of the budget for war. Money for social reforms, money to insure internal development and prosperity is lacking. No progress is made. France suffers and is exhausted. A general uneasiness obstructs commercial and industrial activity. A crisis is near. A collapse is probable.

The solution to avoid catastrophe?

Peace, peace solidly and definitively established.

The means to assure the peace of the world?

Franco-German Understanding

For fear of Germany, France made the Triple-Entente.

For fear of the Triple Entente, Germany arms herself ceaselessly.

To establish equilibrium France, Russia and England increase their armaments in proportion.

Menaced by these formidable forces, all the other countries enter the infernal round of armaments.

Thus is being prepared the most horrible slaughter the world has ever known.

15. Calottes were skullcaps worn by certain members of the clergy; the word is being used here as a term of abuse against the Catholic Church, whom the French Left always associated with reaction.

Wisdom demands, then, the Franco-German understanding which will stop the nations in their race to death and will permit the redirecting toward productive ends a part of the sums absorbed in the preparation of war.

What is it that Opposes This Understanding? Economic Antagonism? The Desire for Revenge?

It is proved that the economic interests of France and Germany are more and more closely bound together. It is equally proved that the idea of revenge is repellent to the French people as a whole, and that the Alsatians and Lorrainers themselves regard it as a monstrosity.

We have made the entente with England and only a dozen years ago. England was for the French the "hereditary enemy," "perfidious Albion," which it was necessary to attack and subjugate. Remember the cry of "Aoh Yes!" cast as a slur on the democrats suspected of dreaming of an understanding with England . . . Canada . . . Fashoda . . . Fashoda was a more serious injury for us than Agadir!

We have forgotten; in a few months opinion has been reversed, the entente-cordiale is made, and no one would dare maintain that it was not a great benefit.

Why should not forgetfulness develop in connection with our differences with the Germans?

It is not possible that the remembrance of the war of '70–'71 should hang eternally over the policy of France. Those who by their incitements feed the discord between the two countries are either fools or miserable fishers in troubled water.

Peace is the essential condition of human development.

Nothing in the order of social reforms and of great industrial and commercial achievements will be made unless the peace of the world is assured.

World peace will be assured only by a Franco-German understanding.

CONCLUSION

The next French Chamber ought to have a majority favorable to a Franco-German rapprochement.

Republicans who are zealous for a great and noble Republic; Democrats who dream of giving to the workers greater well-being; merchants who hope to work in calm and security tomorrow; voters, all powerful by virtue of the ballot, force the candidates to show their position on the question, and vote only for those who will agree to bring about this great work of public safety.

Source: "To Republicans," Le Bonnet Rouge, *1913.*

Selected Bibliography

GENERAL HISTORIES

The literature on the July Crisis and the broader origins of World War I is truly vast. This list is limited to works that have appeared in just the last few years.

Beatty, Jack. *The Lost History of 1914: Reconsidering the Year of the Great War.* New York: Bloomsbury USA, 2012.

Clark, Christopher. *The Sleepwalkers: How Europe Went to War in 1914.* New York: Harper Perennial, 2014.

Ham, Paul. *1914: The Year the World Ended.* London: Doubleday UK, 2015.

Hastings, Max. *Catastrophe 1914: Europe Goes to War.* New York: Vintage, 2013.

MacMillan, Margaret. *The Road to 1914: The War that Ended Peace.* New York: Random House, 2014.

Martel, Gordon. *The Month that Changed the World: July 1914.* New York: Oxford University Press, 2014.

McMeekin, Sean. *July 1914: Countdown to War.* New York: Basic Books, 2014.

Otte, T. G. *July Crisis: The World's Descent into War, Summer 1914.* Cambridge: Cambridge University Press, 2014.

AUSTRIA-HUNGARY

Beaver, Jan G. *Collision Course: Franz Conrad von Hötzendorf, Serbia, and the Politics of Preventive War.* Morrisville, NC: Lulu Press, 2009.

Sondhaus, Lawrence. *Franz Conrad von Hötzendorf: Architect of the Apocalypse.* Leiden: Brill, 2000.

Wawro, Geoffrey. *A Mad Catastrophe: The Outbreak of World War I and the Collapse of the Habsburg Empire.* New York: Basic Books, 2014.

Williamson, Samuel. *Austria-Hungary and the Origins of the First World War.* Boston, MA: Bedford-St. Martin's, 1991.

FRANCE

Bourachot, André. *Marshal Joffre: The Triumphs, Failures and Controversies of France's Commander-in-Chief in the Great War.* Barnsley, UK: Pen and Sword, 2014.

Keiger, John F. V. *France and the Origins of the First World War.* New York: St. Martin's, 1983.

———. *Raymond Poincaré.* Cambridge: Cambridge University Press, 1997.

GERMANY

Berghahn, Volker R. *Germany and the Approach of War in 1914.* Boston, MA: Bedford-St. Martin's, 1993.

Clark, Christopher. *Kaiser Wilhelm II.* London: Routledge, 2000.

Jarausch, Konrad. *The Enigmatic Chancellor: Bethmann Hollweg and the Hubris of Imperial Germany.* New Haven, CT: Yale University Press, 1973.

McDonough, Giles. *The Last Kaiser: The Life of Wilhelm II.* London: St. Martin's, 2001.

Mombauer, Annika. *Helmuth von Moltke and the Origins of the First World War.* Cambridge: Cambridge University Press, 2001.

Röhl, John C. G. *Kaiser Wilhelm II: A Concise Life.* Cambridge: Cambridge University Press, 2014.

GREAT BRITAIN

Hattersley, Roy. *David Lloyd George: The Great Outsider.* Boston, MA: Little, Brown, 2010.

Hinsley, F. H. *British Foreign Policy under Sir Edward Grey.* Cambridge: Cambridge University Press, 1977.

Koss, Stephen. *Asquith.* New York: Columbia University Press, 1985.

Steiner, Zara S., and Keith Neilson. *Britain and the Origins of the First World War.* 2nd edition. London: Palgrave Macmillan, 2003.

Waterhouse, Michael. *Edwardian Requiem: A Life of Sir Edward Grey.* London: Biteback, 2013.

ITALY

Bosworth, R. J. B. *Italy and the Approach of the First World War.* London: Palgrave Macmillan, 1983.

OTTOMAN EMPIRE

Aksakal, Mustafa. *The Ottoman Road to War in 1914: The Ottoman Empire and the First World War.* Cambridge: Cambridge University Press, 2010.

RUSSIA

Carter, Miranda. *George, Nicholas and Wilhelm: Three Royal Cousins and the Road to World War I.* New York: Alfred A. Knopf, 2009.

McMeekin, Sean. *The Russian Origins of the First World War.* Cambridge, MA: Belknap, 2013.

Stone, David R. *The Russian Army in the Great War: The Eastern Front, 1914–1917.* Lawrence: Kansas University Press, 2015.

OTHERS

Hall, Richard C. *Bulgaria's Road to the First World War.* Ann Arbor, MI: East European Monographs, 1996.

Hamilton, Richard F., and Holger H. Herwig. *Decisions for War, 1914–1917.* Cambridge: Cambridge University Press, 2004.

Leon, George B. *Greece and the Great Powers, 1914–1917.* Thessaloniki, Greece: Institute for Balkan Studies, 1974.

Torrey, Glenn. *Romania and World War I: A Collection of Studies.* Las Vegas, NV: Histria Books, 1998.

Acknowledgments

There are many hands involved in the development of any Reacting game, and this one is no exception. Special recognition must go to those faculty members who have reviewed the manuscript and/or tested this game in their own courses. These include Nicolas Proctor, Judy Walden, Patrick Coby, Dwight Brautigam, Phil Garland, Zac Smith, Ann Brown Curry, Andrew Goss, Joe Sramek, Tom Cramer, David Meola, Jeff Hyson, Marina Maccari, Christienna Fryar, and Eden McLean. (This is likely not an exhaustive list.) I have personally had the good fortune of running the game in multiple classes made up of excellent students at Ashland University. They threw themselves into their roles, and in the process helped me to identify aspects that needed improvement. These students include Nicholas Bartulovic, Frances Boggs, Ali Brosky, Joshua Davis, Madeleine Emholtz, Devin Hill, Clayton Hrinko, McKenzie Jones, Brennan Kunkel, Catie Lewis, Tyler MacQueen, Doug Martonik, Owen McManus, James Metzger, C. J. Murnane, Jacob Nestle, Justin Politzer, Matthew Reising, Devin Scott, Cameron Taylor, Shelby Teets, Nick Thielman, Nathan Vacha, Madeline Worcester, and Rebecca Young.

CPSIA information can be obtained
at www.ICGtesting.com
Printed in the USA
LVHW101033210820
663744LV00006B/241